SUPER EASY

GLUTEN-FREE

AIR FRYER

COOKBOOK UK

2025

365 days of Simple fuss-free and Mouthwatering British Nourishing Recipes for a Healthy Lifestyle

FELICIA LEE

WARNING-DISCLAIMER:

TABLE OF CONTENTS

Hello there! I'm chuffed you've picked up my Gluten-Free Air Fryer Cookbook. Whether you're a seasoned cook or just starting out, this book is your ticket to creating delicious, gluten-free meals with that perfect crispy finish – all without the faff of traditional frying.

When I first discovered I needed to go gluten-free, I'll admit I was gobsmacked. Would I have to give up my favourite crispy foods? Would cooking become a right pain? Then I got my hands on an air fryer, and cor blimey, what a game-changer!

This nifty little appliance has revolutionised the way I cook. It's helped me create scrummy, crispy dishes without excessive oil or gluten-containing ingredients. And the best part? It's a doddle to use, even if you're a complete novice in the kitchen.

In this cookbook, I'll guide you through the ins and outs of gluten-free air frying. We'll start with the basics – how to use your air fryer, essential gluten-free ingredients, and simple techniques that'll have you cooking like a pro in no time. Then, we'll dive into a variety of recipes that cater to all tastes and occasions, from quick breakfasts to posh dinner party mains.

Each recipe has been carefully crafted and tested to ensure it's not only gluten-free but also packed with flavour. I've used ingredients that are easy to find in UK shops, and I've included tips and tricks to help you get the best results every time.

Why Gluten-Free?

For those of you who are new to the gluten-free lifestyle, let me explain why it's important. Gluten is a protein found in wheat, barley, and rye. For people with coeliac disease or gluten sensitivity, consuming gluten can lead to a range of health issues. Even if you don't have these conditions, many people find they feel better when they reduce or eliminate gluten from their diet.

Going gluten-free doesn't mean you have to compromise on taste or texture. With the right ingredients and techniques – and a trusty air fryer – you can create meals that are every bit as delicious as their gluten-containing counterparts.

Why Air Frying?

Air frying is a brilliant cooking method, especially for those following a gluten-free diet. Here's why:

1. Healthier Cooking: Air fryers use hot air circulation to cook food, requiring little to no oil. This means you can enjoy crispy, "fried" foods with significantly less fat.

2. Crispy Textures: One of the challenges of gluten-free cooking is achieving that satisfying crunch. Air fryers excel at creating crispy exteriors, perfect for breaded or battered dishes.

3. Versatility: From chips to cakes, air fryers can handle a wide range of recipes. They're great for reheating leftovers too!

4. Time-Saving: Air fryers generally cook faster than conventional ovens, making them perfect for quick meals.

5. Energy Efficient: Using less energy than a full-sized oven, air fryers are a more eco-friendly option for small to medium-sized meals.

How to Use This Cookbook

This cookbook is designed to be your go-to resource for gluten-free air frying. Here's how to make the most of it:

1. Read the "Getting Started" and "Gluten-Free Basics" sections: Even if you're familiar with air fryers or gluten-free cooking, these sections contain valuable information specific to combining these two approaches.

2. Start simple: If you're new to air frying or gluten-free cooking, begin with the easier recipes and work your way up.

3. Don't be afraid to experiment: Once you're comfortable with the basics, feel free to tweak recipes to suit your tastes.

4. Use the menu planning and meal prep sections: These will help you incorporate gluten-free air fryer meals into your daily life efficiently.

5. Pay attention to the nutritional information: This can be particularly helpful if you're managing other dietary needs alongside being gluten-free.

Remember, cooking should be enjoyable. If something doesn't turn out quite right the first time, don't get your knickers in a twist. Practice makes perfect, and before you know it, you'll be whipping up gluten-free air fryer meals like a pro.

So, pop the kettle on, get comfy, and let's embark on this gluten-free air frying journey together. I promise you're in for a treat!

Happy cooking!

What is an Air Fryer?

When I first heard about air fryers, I thought, "Blimey, another kitchen gadget?" But let me tell you, this isn't just any old appliance. An air fryer is a compact countertop convection oven that circulates hot air around food to cook it. It's like having a mini fan oven that can crisp up your food without drowning it in oil.

The beauty of an air fryer is that it can replicate the results of deep-frying with only a fraction of the oil. This means you can enjoy your favourite crispy foods - from chips to chicken - with less fat and fewer calories. Brilliant, right?

How Does an Air Fryer Work?

Now, I'm no scientist, but I'll do my best to explain how this marvellous machine works. At the top of the air fryer, there's a heating mechanism and a fan. When you turn it on, hot air rushes down and around the food placed in the fryer-style basket. This rapid circulation makes the food crisp - similar to deep-frying, but without all the oil.

The temperature and time can be adjusted on the machine, usually between 100°C and 200°C, depending on what you're cooking. Most air fryers also have a shake reminder, which tells you when to shake the basket to ensure even cooking.

Choosing the Right Air Fryer

When I was in the market for an air fryer, I felt a bit like a kid in a sweet shop - there were so many options! Here are a few things to consider when choosing your air fryer:

1. Size: Think about how many people you usually cook for. Air fryers come in various sizes, from small ones perfect for one or two people, to larger ones that can feed a family.

2. Features: Some air fryers come with extra functions like roasting, baking, or dehydrating. Consider which features you'll actually use.

3. Controls: Look for an air fryer with intuitive controls. Some have digital displays, while others use dials.

4. Cleaning: Check if the parts are dishwasher safe for easy cleaning.

5. Price: Air fryers range from budget-friendly to high-end. Remember, the most expensive isn't always the best for your needs.

I ended up choosing a mid-range model with a digital display and a 3.5-litre capacity, which is perfect for my household of two. But your needs might be different, so have a good think about what will work best for you.

Air Fryer Safety Tips

Right, let's talk safety. Air fryers are generally very safe to use, but there are a few things to keep in mind:

1. Read the manual: I know it's tempting to dive right in, but please read the instructions first. Each model is a bit different.

2. Use in a well-ventilated area: Air fryers can get quite hot, so make sure there's plenty of space around it for air to circulate.

3. Don't overfill: Resist the urge to cram in as much food as possible. Overfilling can lead to uneven cooking and potentially damage your air fryer.

4. Be careful of steam: When you open the basket, hot steam will escape. Open it away from you to avoid burns.

5. Use proper utensils: Avoid metal utensils that could scratch the non-stick coating. Silicone or wooden utensils are best.

6. Unplug when not in use: Always unplug your air fryer when you're done using it.

Cleaning and Maintenance

Keeping your air fryer clean is crucial for both hygiene and longevity. Here's how I keep mine in tip-top shape:

1. Clean after each use: Once the air fryer has cooled, wipe the inside with a damp cloth or sponge.

2. Wash removable parts: The basket and pan can usually be washed with warm, soapy water or put in the dishwasher if they're dishwasher safe.

3. Deep clean occasionally: Every few uses, give your air fryer a thorough clean. Soak the removable parts in hot, soapy water and clean the heating element with a soft brush.

4. Avoid abrasive cleaners: These can damage the non-stick coating.

5. Dry thoroughly: Make sure all parts are completely dry before reassembling and storing.

Essential Accessories

While your air fryer will come with everything you need to get started, there are a few accessories that I've found really useful:

1. Oil sprayer: This helps you add just a light coating of oil to your food for extra crispiness.

2. Parchment paper liners: These make cleaning even easier and can prevent delicate foods from sticking.

3. Silicone tongs: Perfect for flipping food without scratching the basket.

4. Extra baskets: If you're cooking for a family, having an extra basket can be handy for cooking different foods simultaneously.

5. Baking pan: Some recipes work better in a solid pan rather than the perforated basket.

Converting Traditional Recipes for the Air Fryer

One of the things I love about my air fryer is how versatile it is. You can convert many traditional recipes for air frying with a few simple adjustments:

1. Temperature: Generally, reduce the temperature by about 25°C compared to conventional oven recipes.

2. Time: Air fryers usually cook faster than conventional ovens. Start by reducing the cooking time by about 20% and check for doneness.

3. Oil: You'll need much less oil in an air fryer. A light spray or brush of oil is usually enough.

4. Size: Cut ingredients into smaller, even pieces for faster and more even cooking.

5. Don't overcrowd: Cook in batches if necessary to ensure proper air circulation.

6. Shake or flip: For even cooking, shake the basket or flip food halfway through cooking.

Remember, these are general guidelines. It might take a bit of trial and error to get your favourite recipes just right in the air fryer. But don't worry – even the "failures" are usually still pretty tasty!

With these basics under your belt, you're well on your way to becoming an air frying pro. In the next section, we'll dive into the specifics of gluten-free cooking. Get ready to combine your new air frying skills with delicious gluten-free ingredients for some truly scrummy meals!

Welcome to the world of gluten-free cooking! If you're new to this, don't worry – I've got your back. When I first started my gluten-free journey, I felt a bit lost. But with some practice and the right knowledge, I've found that gluten-free cooking can be just as delicious and even more creative than traditional cooking. Let's dive in!

Understanding Gluten

First things first – what exactly is gluten? Gluten is a protein found in wheat, barley, and rye. It's what gives bread its chewy texture and helps it rise. For people with coeliac disease or gluten sensitivity, consuming gluten can cause a range of health issues.

In the UK, you'll find gluten in lots of common foods:
- Bread, pasta, and baked goods
- Many breakfast cereals
- Beer and some other alcoholic drinks
- Many sauces and gravies
- Some processed meats

Essential Gluten-Free Ingredients

When I first went gluten-free, I was chuffed to discover how many naturally gluten-free ingredients there are. Here are some staples I always keep in my kitchen:

1. Gluten-free flours: Rice flour, almond flour, coconut flour, chickpea flour
2. Gluten-free grains: Rice, quinoa, millet, buckwheat (despite the name, it's gluten-free!)
3. Starches: Cornstarch, potato starch, tapioca starch
4. Xanthan gum: This helps bind gluten-free baked goods
5. Gluten-free oats: Regular oats can be contaminated, so look for certified gluten-free
6. Nuts and seeds: Great for snacking and adding crunch to dishes

7. Fresh fruits and vegetables: All naturally gluten-free!

Reading Labels

Learning to read labels is crucial when you're eating gluten-free. In the UK, allergens (including gluten) must be clearly labelled on food packaging. Look out for these terms:
- Wheat
- Barley
- Rye
- Oats (unless specified as gluten-free)

- Malt
- Spelt

Be careful with terms like "wheat-free" – this doesn't necessarily mean gluten-free. Always look for products specifically labelled as gluten-free.

Cross-Contamination

When you're cooking gluten-free, it's important to avoid cross-contamination. This is especially crucial if you're cooking for someone with coeliac disease. Here are some tips:

1. Use separate chopping boards, utensils, and toasters for gluten-free foods
2. Clean surfaces thoroughly before preparing gluten-free foods
3. Use separate spreads, jams, and condiments to avoid crumb contamination
4. When eating out, always inform the staff about your gluten-free needs

Gluten-Free Baking

Baking was the trickiest part for me when I went gluten-free. Without gluten, baked goods can turn out dry, crumbly, or dense. But don't worry – with a few tricks up your sleeve, you can create delicious gluten-free bakes:

1. Use a gluten-free flour blend: These are designed to mimic the properties of wheat flour
2. Add xanthan gum: This helps bind the ingredients and improve texture
3. Increase leavening agents: Gluten-free bakes often need more baking powder or bicarbonate of soda
4. Add moisture: Gluten-free flours tend to absorb more liquid, so you might need to add extra eggs, oil, or milk
5. Don't overmix: This can lead to a tough texture

Gluten-Free Substitutes

There are loads of brilliant gluten-free substitutes available these days. Here are some of my favourites:

- Pasta: Try pasta made from rice, corn, or legumes
- Bread: Look for loaves made with gluten-free flours or try making your own
- Crackers: Rice cakes or gluten-free crackers are great alternatives
- Beer: There are many tasty gluten-free beers on the market now
- Soy sauce: Tamari is a great gluten-free alternative

Adapting Recipes

When you're adapting traditional recipes to be gluten-free, keep these tips in mind:

1. Substitute flours: Use a gluten-free flour blend in place of wheat flour
2. Adjust liquids: You might need to add more liquid to your recipe
3. Be mindful of binding: Add xanthan gum or an extra egg if needed
4. Consider texture: Gluten-free bakes might need extra ingredients like nuts or dried fruit for texture
5. Be patient: It might take a few tries to get a recipe just right

Gluten-Free Air Frying Tips

Now, let's talk about combining gluten-free cooking with air frying. It's a match made in heaven, I tell you! Here are some tips I've learned:

1. Use gluten-free breadcrumbs: You can make your own from gluten-free bread or buy ready-made ones
2. Try alternative coatings: Crushed nuts, seeds, or gluten-free cereals make great crispy coatings
3. Don't skip the oil: A light spray of oil helps gluten-free coatings crisp up nicely
4. Preheat your air fryer: This helps achieve a crispy exterior
5. Don't overcrowd: Cook in batches for the best results

Troubleshooting Common Gluten-Free Cooking Issues

Even with the best intentions, things can sometimes go pear-shaped. Here are some common issues and how to fix them:

1. Dry baked goods: Add more liquid or fat to your recipe
2. Crumbly texture: Try adding an extra egg or some xanthan gum
3. Dense results: Make sure you're not overmixing and try adding a bit more leavening agent
4. Gritty texture: Try using a finer ground flour or letting your batter rest before cooking

Remember, practice makes perfect. Don't be discouraged if your first few attempts aren't spot on. Keep at it, and soon you'll be whipping up delicious gluten-free meals like a pro!

When I first went gluten-free, I found myself standing in front of the fridge, scratching my head about what to eat. That's when I realized the importance of menu planning and meal prep. Trust me, a little planning goes a long way in making gluten-free living a breeze!

Benefits of Menu Planning

1. Saves time: No more last-minute panic about what to cook
2. Saves money: Less impulse buying and food waste
3. Ensures balanced meals: You can plan to include a variety of nutrients
4. Reduces stress: Knowing what's for dinner is a real relief!

How to Plan Your Menu

Here's my weekly routine for menu planning:
1. Check your schedule: Look at the week ahead. Are there any busy nights when you'll need quick meals?
2. Take stock: Check what you already have in your pantry and fridge
3. Plan your meals: I usually plan for 5-6 days, leaving room for leftovers or takeaways
4. Make a shopping list: Based on your meal plan, list what you need to buy
5. Be flexible: It's okay to swap meals around if your plans change

Sample Weekly Menu

Here's an example of how I might plan my week:
- Monday: Air Fryer Gluten-Free Chicken Nuggets with Sweet Potato Fries
- Tuesday: Quinoa Stir-Fry with Vegetables
- Wednesday: Air Fryer Fish and Chips
- Thursday: Gluten-Free Pasta with Homemade Pesto
- Friday: Air Fryer Stuffed Bell Peppers
- Saturday: Leftovers or Takeaway
- Sunday: Roast Dinner with Air Fryer Roast Potatoes

Meal Prep Basics

Meal prep can be a game-changer when you're eating gluten-free. Here's how I approach it:
1. Choose a prep day: I like Sunday afternoons, but pick a time that works for you
2. Start with the basics: Cook large batches of grains, roast vegetables, and prepare proteins
3. Prep ingredients: Wash and chop vegetables, make sauces or dressings
4. Cook in batches: Use your air fryer to cook multiple servings at once
5. Store properly: Invest in good quality, airtight containers

Air Fryer Meal Prep Tips

Your air fryer can be a brilliant tool for meal prep. Here are some tips:
1. Cook in batches: Most air fryers can cook enough for 2-3 servings at a time
2. Use it for multiple components: You can cook your protein and sides in the air fryer
3. Reheat leftovers: The air fryer is great for crisping up leftovers
4. Prep snacks: Make a batch of air fryer roasted nuts or chickpeas for the week

Storing and Reheating Gluten-Free Air Fryer Meals

Proper storage is key to successful meal prep:
1. Cool before storing: Let food cool to room temperature before refrigerating
2. Use airtight containers: This prevents cross-contamination and keeps food fresh
3. Label everything: Include the dish name and date it was prepared
4. Reheat safely: Use your air fryer to reheat meals for the best texture

Remember, most prepared meals will keep in the fridge for 3-4 days. If you've made extra, pop it in the freezer for future use.

Quick and Easy Gluten-Free Air Fryer Meals

Sometimes, even with the best planning, you need a quick meal. Here are some of my go-to quick gluten-free air fryer meals:

1. Air Fryer Omelette: Whisk eggs with your favourite fillings, pour into a small baking dish, and air fry for a quick breakfast or lunch
2. Gluten-Free Pizza: Use a gluten-free base, top as desired, and air fry for a crispy crust
3. Air Fryer Fajitas: Slice chicken and peppers, season, and air fry. Serve with gluten-free tortillas
4. Stuffed Sweet Potatoes: Air fry sweet potatoes, then top with your favourite fillings
5. Air Fryer Salmon: Season a salmon fillet and air fry for a quick, healthy dinner

With these menu planning and meal prep tips, you'll find that gluten-free living with your air fryer can be both delicious and stress-free. Happy planning!

 Nutritional Information

When I first went gluten-free, I was worried about missing out on important nutrients. But with a bit of knowledge and planning, a gluten-free diet can be just as nutritious – if not more so – than a traditional diet. Let's dive into the nutritional aspects of gluten-free eating.

Understanding Nutritional Needs

Everyone's nutritional needs are different, but generally, we all need a balance of:

1. Carbohydrates: For energy

2. Proteins: For growth and repair

3. Fats: For hormone production and nutrient absorption

4. Vitamins and Minerals: For various bodily functions

5. Fibre: For digestive health

When you go gluten-free, you might need to pay extra attention to certain nutrients.

Nutrients to Watch

When following a gluten-free diet, keep an eye on these nutrients:

1. Fibre: Many gluten-free alternatives are lower in fibre. Include plenty of fruits, vegetables, and gluten-free whole grains.

2. B Vitamins: Especially B1 (Thiamin), B2 (Riboflavin), B3 (Niacin), and Folate. These are often added to wheat-based products but not always to gluten-free alternatives.

3. Iron: Wheat flour is often fortified with iron. Make sure you're getting enough from other sources like lean meats, legumes, and leafy greens.

4. Calcium: If you've cut out certain grains, you might be getting less calcium. Dairy products (if tolerated), leafy greens, and fortified non-dairy milks are good sources.

5. Magnesium: Found in whole grains, nuts, and seeds.

Reading Nutrition Labels

Understanding nutrition labels is crucial for maintaining a balanced gluten-free diet. Here's what to look for:

1. Serving Size: All nutritional information is based on this amount

2. Calories: Important if you're watching your weight

3. Macronutrients: Carbohydrates, Protein, and Fat

4. Fibre: Aim for foods higher in fibre

5. Vitamins and Minerals: Look for foods fortified with B vitamins and iron

6. Ingredients List: Check for hidden sources of gluten

Balancing Your Plate

A balanced gluten-free meal should include:

1. Gluten-free carbohydrates: Such as rice, quinoa, potatoes, or gluten-free bread

2. Lean protein: Like chicken, fish, tofu, or legumes

3. Fruits and vegetables: Aim for a variety of colours

4. Healthy fats: From sources like olive oil, avocados, or nuts

Nutritional Benefits of Air Frying

Air frying can be a healthier cooking method compared to traditional frying:

1. Lower in fat: Air frying typically uses much less oil

2. Fewer calories: Due to the reduced oil use

3. Retains nutrients: The quick cooking time can help preserve heat-sensitive vitamins

Nutritional Considerations for Gluten-Free Air Fryer Recipes

When using your air fryer for gluten-free cooking, keep these nutritional tips in mind:

1. Use whole grain gluten-free flours: For breading or batters, try almond flour or gluten-free oat flour for added nutrients

2. Include a variety of vegetables: Air frying is great for cooking vegetables quickly while retaining their nutrients

3. Choose lean proteins: Air frying can help cook proteins with less added fat

4. Be mindful of added fats: While air frying uses less oil, be aware of high-fat ingredients in your recipes

5. Watch portion sizes: Air fried foods can be delicious, making it easy to overeat

Sample Nutritional Information

Here's an example of how I might present nutritional information for a recipe in this cookbook:

Air Fryer Gluten-Free Chicken Nuggets (Serves 4)

- Calories: 250 per serving

- Protein: 20g

- Carbohydrates: 15g

- Fat: 12g

- Fibre: 3g

- Iron: 10% of Daily Value

- Vitamin B3 (Niacin): 25% of Daily Value

Remember, these values are approximate and can vary based on specific ingredients and brands used.

Consulting a Professional

While this information provides a general guide, it's always a good idea to consult with a registered dietitian or your healthcare provider, especially if you have specific health concerns or nutritional needs. They can provide personalized advice to ensure you're meeting all your nutritional requirements on a gluten-free diet.

By paying attention to your nutritional needs and making informed choices, you can enjoy a varied, delicious, and nutritious gluten-free diet with your air fryer. Here's to your health!

FULL ENGLISH BREAKFAST STACK

Prep: 10 mins | Cook: 25 mins | Serves: 2

Ingredients:

- **UK:** 4 gluten-free sausages, 4 rashers of bacon, 4 large mushrooms, 2 eggs, 100g cherry tomatoes, 1 gluten-free hash brown

Instructions:

1. Preheat the air fryer to 180°C (350°F).
2. Place sausages and bacon in the air fryer basket. Air fry for 10 minutes, turning halfway.
3. Add mushrooms and hash browns, cooking for another 10 minutes until golden and crispy.
4. While that cooks, crack eggs into individual air fryer-safe dishes. Add cherry tomatoes around the eggs.
5. Air fry the eggs and tomatoes for 5 minutes or until the eggs reach your desired doneness.
6. Assemble your breakfast stack, layering each component. Serve hot.

Nutritional Info: Calories: 500 | Fat: 35g | Carbs: 12g | Protein: 30g

CRISPY HASH BROWNS

Prep: 10 mins | Cook: 15 mins | Serves: 4

Ingredients:

- **UK:** 500g potatoes (peeled and grated), 1 small onion (finely chopped), 1 egg, salt, pepper, 1 tablespoon olive oil

Instructions:

1. Preheat air fryer to 180°C (350°F).
2. In a bowl, mix the grated potatoes, onion, egg, salt, and pepper.
3. Form into patties and brush with olive oil.
4. Place the patties in the air fryer basket in a single layer. Air fry for 10-15 minutes, flipping halfway, until golden and crispy.
5. Serve your gluten-free hash browns as a side or a breakfast staple.

Nutritional Info: Calories: 220 | Fat: 8g | Carbs: 30g | Protein: 4g

CHEESY SPINACH AND MUSHROOM FRITTATA

Prep: 5 mins | Cook: 15 mins | Serves: 4

Ingredients:

- **UK:** 6 eggs, 100g spinach (chopped), 100g mushrooms (sliced), 50g cheddar cheese (grated), 1 tablespoon olive oil, salt, pepper

Instructions:

1. Preheat air fryer to 160°C (320°F).
2. In a bowl, whisk eggs, then stir in spinach, mushrooms, cheese, salt, and pepper.
3. Grease an air fryer-safe dish with olive oil. Pour the egg mixture into the dish.
4. Air fry for 12-15 minutes, until the frittata is set and golden on top.
5. Slice and serve your cheesy spinach and mushroom frittata.

Nutritional Info: Calories: 180 | Fat: 14g | Carbs: 3g | Protein: 12g

CINNAMON APPLE BREAKFAST CRISPS

Prep: 5 mins | Cook: 10 mins | Serves: 2

Ingredients:

- **UK:** 2 apples (thinly sliced), 1 teaspoon ground cinnamon, 1 tablespoon honey

Instructions:

1. Preheat air fryer to 170°C (340°F).
2. Toss apple slices in cinnamon and honey until well coated.
3. Spread the apples in a single layer in the air fryer basket.
4. Air fry for 8-10 minutes, flipping halfway through, until crispy.
5. Serve as a sweet, crunchy breakfast snack or topping.

Nutritional Info: Calories: 120 | Fat: 0g | Carbs: 32g | Protein: 1g

GLUTEN-FREE CRUMPETS

Prep: 15 mins | Cook: 10 mins | Serves: 4

Ingredients:

- **UK:** 150g gluten-free flour, 250ml warm water, 1 teaspoon yeast, 1 teaspoon sugar, 1/2 teaspoon salt, 1 tablespoon olive oil

Instructions:

1. In a bowl, mix the yeast, sugar, and warm water. Let it sit for 10 minutes until frothy.
2. Stir in gluten-free flour and salt until you have a smooth batter. Let it rest for 30 minutes.
3. Preheat air fryer to 180°C (350°F).
4. Grease crumpet rings and place them in the air fryer. Pour batter into each ring, filling halfway.
5. Air fry for 10 minutes, or until the crumpets are golden and cooked through.
6. Serve hot with butter or your favourite toppings.

Nutritional Info: Calories: 150 | Fat: 4g | Carbs: 26g | Protein: 3g

BACON AND EGG CUPS

Prep: 5 mins | Cook: 10 mins | Serves: 4

Ingredients:

- **UK:** 4 rashers of bacon, 4 eggs, salt, pepper

Instructions:

1. Preheat air fryer to 180°C (350°F).
2. Line each section of an air fryer-safe muffin tin with a rasher of bacon.
3. Crack an egg into each bacon-lined cup and season with salt and pepper.
4. Air fry for 8-10 minutes, until the eggs are cooked to your liking.
5. Serve your bacon and egg cups as a simple, hearty breakfast.

Nutritional Info: Calories: 200 | Fat: 15g | Carbs: 1g | Protein: 15g

SWEET POTATO AND KALE BREAKFAST HASH

Prep: 10 mins | Cook: 15 mins | Serves: 4

Ingredients:

- **UK:** 300g sweet potato (diced), 100g kale (chopped), 1 onion (chopped), 1 tablespoon olive oil, salt, pepper

Instructions:

1. Preheat air fryer to 180°C (350°F).
2. Toss the sweet potato, kale, and onion with olive oil, salt, and pepper.
3. Place in the air fryer basket and cook for 12-15 minutes, shaking halfway through.
4. Serve as a nutritious breakfast side or as part of a full meal.

Nutritional Info: Calories: 180 | Fat: 7g | Carbs: 24g | Protein: 3g

BERRY AND OAT BREAKFAST BARS

Prep: 10 mins | Cook: 12 mins | Serves: 6

Ingredients:

- **UK:** 200g gluten-free oats, 100g mixed berries, 50g honey, 2 tablespoons peanut butter, 1 teaspoon vanilla extract

Instructions:

1. Preheat air fryer to 160°C (320°F).
2. Mix the oats, berries, honey, peanut butter, and vanilla in a bowl.
3. Press the mixture into a greased air fryer-safe tray.
4. Air fry for 10-12 minutes, until golden and firm.
5. Let cool, then slice into bars. Enjoy for a quick breakfast on the go.

Nutritional Info: Calories: 220 | Fat: 7g | Carbs: 36g | Protein: 6g

SMOKED SALMON AND DILL FRITTATA

Prep: 5 mins | Cook: 12 mins | Serves: 2

Ingredients:

- **UK:** 4 eggs, 50g smoked salmon, 1 tablespoon fresh dill, salt, pepper

Instructions:

1. Preheat air fryer to 160°C (320°F).
2. In a bowl, whisk the eggs and stir in smoked salmon, dill, salt, and pepper.
3. Pour the mixture into an air fryer-safe dish.
4. Air fry for 10-12 minutes, until the frittata is set and cooked through.
5. Serve with a sprinkle of fresh dill on top.

Nutritional Info: Calories: 200 | Fat: 14g | Carbs: 1g | Protein: 18g

GLUTEN-FREE BREAKFAST SAUSAGE PATTIES

Prep: 10 mins | Cook: 10 mins | Serves: 4

Ingredients:

- **UK:** 500g minced pork, 1 teaspoon sage, 1 teaspoon thyme, 1/2 teaspoon garlic powder, salt, pepper

Instructions:

1. Preheat air fryer to 180°C (350°F).
2. In a bowl, mix minced pork with sage, thyme, garlic powder, salt, and pepper.
3. Form into small patties and place them in the air fryer.
4. Air fry for 8-10 minutes, flipping halfway through, until the patties are browned and cooked through.
5. Serve with eggs or as part of a full breakfast.

Nutritional Info: Calories: 280 | Fat: 22g | Carbs: 1g | Protein: 20g

CRISPY HALLOUMI FRIES

Prep: 5 mins | Cook: 10 mins | Serves: 4

Ingredients:

- **UK:** 250g halloumi (cut into fries), 30g gluten-free flour, 1 tsp paprika, 1 tsp garlic powder, olive oil spray, lemon wedges (to serve)

Instructions:

1. Preheat the air fryer to 180°C.
2. In a bowl, mix the gluten-free flour, paprika, and garlic powder.
3. Coat the halloumi fries in the seasoned flour.
4. Lightly spray the air fryer basket with olive oil. Place the halloumi fries in a single layer, spraying them with a little more olive oil.
5. Air fry for 8-10 minutes, turning halfway, until golden and crispy.
6. Serve with lemon wedges for a zesty finish.

Nutritional Info: Calories: 200 | Fat: 15g | Carbs: 5g | Protein: 13g

SPICY CHICKPEA POPPERS

Prep: 10 mins | Cook: 12 mins | Serves: 4

Ingredients:

- **UK:** 400g tin chickpeas (drained and rinsed), 2 tbsp olive oil, 1 tsp smoked paprika, 1/2 tsp cayenne pepper, salt, pepper

Instructions:

1. Preheat the air fryer to 190°C.
2. In a bowl, toss the chickpeas with olive oil, smoked paprika, cayenne pepper, salt, and pepper until evenly coated.
3. Place the chickpeas in the air fryer basket in a single layer.
4. Cook for 10-12 minutes, shaking halfway through, until crispy and golden.
5. Let the chickpeas cool slightly before serving—they crisp up further as they cool.

Nutritional Info: Calories: 120 | Fat: 5g | Carbs: 14g | Protein: 5g

GLUTEN-FREE SAUSAGE ROLLS

Prep: 15 mins | Cook: 20 mins | Serves: 6

Ingredients:

- **UK:** 500g gluten-free puff pastry, 300g gluten-free sausage meat, 1 tsp dried sage, 1 egg (beaten), salt, pepper

Instructions:

1. Preheat the air fryer to 180°C.
2. Roll out the puff pastry and cut into strips wide enough to wrap around the sausage meat.
3. Mix the sausage meat with dried sage, salt, and pepper. Form into sausage shapes and place in the middle of the pastry strips.
4. Roll the pastry around the sausage meat, sealing the edges with a little beaten egg.
5. Place the sausage rolls in the air fryer basket, brush with egg, and cook for 18-20 minutes, until golden and crispy.
6. Let them cool slightly before serving.

Nutritional Info: Calories: 300 | Fat: 20g | Carbs: 22g | Protein: 10g

CRISPY VEGETABLE PAKORAS

Prep: 10 mins | Cook: 15 mins | Serves: 4

Ingredients:

- **UK:** 100g chickpea flour, 1 tsp ground cumin, 1/2 tsp turmeric, 1/2 tsp chilli powder, 1 small onion (thinly sliced), 1 small potato (grated), 50g spinach (chopped), 2 tbsp water, salt, olive oil spray

Instructions:

1. Preheat the air fryer to 180°C.
2. In a bowl, mix chickpea flour, cumin, turmeric, chilli powder, and salt. Add the sliced onion, grated potato, and spinach.
3. Gradually add water to form a thick batter.
4. Scoop spoonfuls of the batter into the air fryer basket, forming small fritters.
5. Spray with olive oil and air fry for 12-15 minutes, turning halfway, until crispy and golden.
6. Serve hot with a chutney or dipping sauce.

Nutritional Info: Calories: 180 | Fat: 5g | Carbs: 28g | Protein: 6g

GARLIC AND HERB MUSHROOMS

Prep: 5 mins | Cook: 8 mins | Serves: 4

Ingredients:

- **UK:** 300g button mushrooms, 2 tbsp olive oil, 1 tsp garlic powder, 1 tsp dried thyme, salt, pepper

Instructions:

1. Preheat the air fryer to 180°C.
2. Toss the mushrooms with olive oil, garlic powder, dried thyme, salt, and pepper.
3. Place the mushrooms in the air fryer basket in a single layer.
4. Cook for 8 minutes, shaking halfway, until golden and tender.
5. Serve as a snack or side dish, garnished with fresh herbs if desired.

Nutritional Info: Calories: 90 | Fat: 7g | Carbs: 4g | Protein: 3g

HOMEMADE POTATO CRISPS WITH SEA SALT AND VINEGAR

Prep: 10 mins | Cook: 15 mins | Serves: 4

Ingredients:

- **UK:** 2 large potatoes (thinly sliced), 1 tbsp olive oil, 2 tbsp malt vinegar, sea salt to taste

Instructions:

1. Preheat the air fryer to 170°C.
2. Toss the potato slices in olive oil and malt vinegar.
3. Place the slices in a single layer in the air fryer basket and cook for 12-15 minutes, shaking every few minutes to ensure even cooking.
4. Once crispy, sprinkle with sea salt and serve immediately.

Nutritional Info: Calories: 150 | Fat: 5g | Carbs: 22g | Protein: 2g

CRISPY COCONUT PRAWNS

Prep: 10 mins | Cook: 10 mins | Serves: 4

Ingredients:

- **UK:** 250g large prawns (peeled and deveined), 50g desiccated coconut, 50g gluten-free breadcrumbs, 1 egg (beaten), salt, pepper, olive oil spray

Instructions:

1. Preheat the air fryer to 190°C.
2. In a bowl, mix desiccated coconut and gluten-free breadcrumbs. Season with salt and pepper.
3. Dip each prawn into the beaten egg, then coat in the coconut mixture.
4. Arrange the prawns in a single layer in the air fryer basket and spray lightly with olive oil.
5. Cook for 8-10 minutes, flipping halfway, until golden and crispy.
6. Serve with a sweet chilli dipping sauce.

Nutritional Info: Calories: 200 | Fat: 10g | Carbs: 12g | Protein: 16g

STUFFED JALAPEÑO POPPERS

Prep: 10 mins | Cook: 10 mins | Serves: 4

Ingredients:

- **UK:** 6 large jalapeños (halved and deseeded), 100g cream cheese, 50g cheddar cheese (grated), 50g gluten-free breadcrumbs, 1 tsp smoked paprika, olive oil spray

Instructions:

1. Preheat the air fryer to 180°C.
2. In a bowl, mix the cream cheese, grated cheddar, and smoked paprika.
3. Fill each jalapeño half with the cheese mixture and top with gluten-free breadcrumbs.
4. Place the stuffed jalapeños in the air fryer basket and spray with olive oil.
5. Air fry for 8-10 minutes, until the breadcrumbs are golden and crispy.
6. Serve immediately.

Nutritional Info: Calories: 160 | Fat: 12g | Carbs: 8g | Protein: 5g

GLUTEN-FREE ONION BHAJIS

Prep: 10 mins | Cook: 12 mins | Serves: 4

Ingredients:

- **UK:** 2 large onions (thinly sliced), 100g chickpea flour, 1 tsp ground cumin, 1/2 tsp turmeric, 1/2 tsp chilli powder, 2 tbsp water, salt, olive oil spray

Instructions:

1. Preheat the air fryer to 180°C.
2. In a bowl, mix the chickpea flour, cumin, turmeric, chilli powder, and salt. Add the sliced onions and water to form a thick batter.
3. Scoop spoonfuls of the mixture into the air fryer basket.
4. Spray with olive oil and air fry for 10-12 minutes, turning halfway, until golden and crispy.
5. Serve with a yoghurt dip or chutney.

Nutritional Info: Calories: 160 | Fat: 4g | Carbs: 25g | Protein: 4g

SWEET AND SPICY MIXED NUTS

Prep: 5 mins | Cook: 10 mins | Serves: 4

Ingredients:

- **UK:** 200g mixed nuts (almonds, cashews, pecans), 2 tbsp maple syrup, 1 tsp cinnamon, 1/2 tsp cayenne pepper, sea salt

Instructions:

1. Preheat the air fryer to 160°C.
2. In a bowl, toss the mixed nuts with maple syrup, cinnamon, cayenne pepper, and a pinch of sea salt.
3. Place the nuts in the air fryer basket in a single layer.
4. Cook for 8-10 minutes, shaking halfway, until toasted and caramelised.
5. Let cool before serving.

Nutritional Info: Calories: 220 | Fat: 18g | Carbs: 12g | Protein: 6g

GLUTEN-FREE AIR FRYER BREAD

Prep: 15 mins | Cook: 45 mins | Serves: 1 loaf

Ingredients:

- **UK:** 300g gluten-free flour blend, 10g instant yeast, 1 tablespoon sugar, 1 teaspoon salt, 250ml warm water, 30ml olive oil, 1 egg (beaten)

Instructions:

1. In a bowl, mix the gluten-free flour, yeast, sugar, and salt.
2. Gradually stir in the warm water, olive oil, and beaten egg until you form a smooth dough.
3. Knead the dough lightly on a floured surface until it becomes elastic.
4. Shape the dough into a loaf and place it in a greased, oven-safe loaf tin that fits your air fryer basket.
5. Set your air fryer to 160°C (320°F) and bake the bread for 40-45 minutes, until it's golden brown on top and sounds hollow when tapped.
6. Let the bread cool on a wire rack before slicing.

Nutritional Info: Calories: 210 | Fat: 8g | Carbs: 32g | Protein: 4g

HERB AND GARLIC FLATBREAD

Prep: 10 mins | Cook: 12 mins | Serves: 4

Ingredients:

- **UK:** 250g gluten-free flour, 1 teaspoon baking powder, 1 teaspoon salt, 150ml warm water, 2 tablespoons olive oil, 1 tablespoon dried mixed herbs, 1 clove garlic (minced)

Instructions:

1. In a bowl, combine the gluten-free flour, baking powder, and salt.
2. Slowly add the warm water and olive oil, mixing until a soft dough forms.
3. Stir in the minced garlic and herbs.
4. Divide the dough into four balls and flatten each into a flatbread shape.
5. Preheat the air fryer to 180°C (350°F) and cook the flatbreads for 6 minutes on each side, flipping halfway.
6. Serve warm with dips or as a side to your main meal.

Nutritional Info: Calories: 140 | Fat: 5g | Carbs: 20g | Protein: 2g

GLUTEN-FREE BANANA BREAD

Prep: 10 mins | Cook: 40 mins | Serves: 1 loaf

Ingredients:

- **UK:** 200g gluten-free flour, 100g sugar, 1 teaspoon baking soda, 1/2 teaspoon salt, 3 ripe bananas (mashed), 2 eggs, 60ml vegetable oil, 1 teaspoon vanilla extract

Instructions:

1. In a large bowl, combine the flour, sugar, baking soda, and salt.
2. In another bowl, whisk together the mashed bananas, eggs, oil, and vanilla extract.
3. Fold the wet ingredients into the dry ingredients until just combined.
4. Pour the mixture into a greased loaf tin that fits in your air fryer.
5. Set your air fryer to 160°C (320°F) and bake for 40 minutes. Use a toothpick to check if it's done (it should come out clean).
6. Let it cool before slicing and enjoying.

Nutritional Info: Calories: 210 | Fat: 9g | Carbs: 30g | Protein: 3g

GARLIC KNOTS

Prep: 20 mins | Cook: 10 mins | Serves: 12 knots

Ingredients:

- **UK:** 250g gluten-free flour, 10g instant yeast, 1 tablespoon sugar, 1 teaspoon salt, 120ml warm water, 2 tablespoons olive oil, 2 cloves garlic (minced), fresh parsley (for garnish)

Instructions:

1. Mix the flour, yeast, sugar, and salt in a bowl.
2. Gradually add warm water and olive oil, forming a soft dough.
3. Roll the dough into small balls, then shape them into knots.
4. Preheat the air fryer to 180°C (350°F) and cook the knots for 8-10 minutes until golden.
5. Toss the warm knots in garlic and olive oil and sprinkle with parsley.

Nutritional Info: Calories: 100 | Fat: 5g | Carbs: 12g | Protein: 2g

ROSEMARY OLIVE OIL FOCACCIA

Prep: 20 mins | Cook: 20 mins | Serves: 6

Ingredients:

- **UK:** 300g gluten-free flour, 10g instant yeast, 1 teaspoon salt, 240ml warm water, 3 tablespoons olive oil, 1 tablespoon fresh rosemary (chopped), sea salt (for sprinkling)

Instructions:

1. Combine flour, yeast, and salt in a bowl.
2. Gradually add warm water and olive oil to form a sticky dough.
3. Flatten the dough into an air fryer-safe baking dish.
4. Drizzle olive oil over the dough and sprinkle with rosemary and sea salt.
5. Air fry at 180°C (350°F) for 15-20 minutes until golden and firm.

Nutritional Info: Calories: 220 | Fat: 9g | Carbs: 28g | Protein: 3g

CINNAMON ROLLS WITH CREAM CHEESE FROSTING

Prep: 20 mins | Cook: 15 mins | Serves: 8 rolls

Ingredients:

- **UK:** 250g gluten-free flour, 10g instant yeast, 50g sugar, 120ml warm milk, 1 egg (beaten), 50g unsalted butter (softened), 2 tablespoons cinnamon, 50g brown sugar
- For the frosting: 60g cream cheese, 30g butter, 60g icing sugar, 1 teaspoon vanilla extract

Instructions:

1. In a large bowl, mix the flour, yeast, and sugar.
2. Add the warm milk, beaten egg, and softened butter to the mixture and form a dough.
3. Roll the dough out into a rectangle and spread softened butter over it. Mix cinnamon and brown sugar together and sprinkle evenly over the dough.
4. Roll the dough tightly into a log and cut into 8 slices.
5. Preheat the air fryer to 170°C (340°F) and place the cinnamon rolls in an air fryer-safe baking tin.
6. Cook for 12-15 minutes until golden and risen.
7. For the frosting, beat together the cream cheese, butter, icing sugar, and vanilla. Spread the frosting over the warm rolls before serving.

Nutritional Info: Calories: 320 | Fat: 15g | Carbs: 42g | Protein: 5g

CHEDDAR BISCUITS

Prep: 10 mins | Cook: 12 mins | Serves: 8 biscuits

Ingredients:

- **UK:** 200g gluten-free self-raising flour, 50g unsalted butter (cold), 100g cheddar cheese (grated), 120ml milk, 1 teaspoon baking powder, pinch of salt

Instructions:

1. In a bowl, rub the cold butter into the flour until the mixture resembles breadcrumbs.
2. Stir in the grated cheddar, baking powder, and salt.
3. Gradually add milk until the dough comes together.
4. Divide the dough into 8 portions and shape into biscuits.
5. Preheat the air fryer to 180°C (350°F) and bake for 10-12 minutes until golden brown and puffed.
6. Serve warm with butter or as a savoury side to soups and stews.

Nutritional Info: Calories: 150 | Fat: 8g | Carbs: 18g | Protein: 4g

PUMPKIN MUFFINS

Prep: 10 mins | Cook: 18 mins | Serves: 12 muffins

Ingredients:

- **UK:** 200g gluten-free flour, 1 teaspoon baking powder, 1/2 teaspoon baking soda, 1 teaspoon cinnamon, 1/2 teaspoon ground nutmeg, 200g pumpkin puree, 100g sugar, 2 eggs, 60ml vegetable oil

Instructions:

1. In a bowl, whisk together the flour, baking powder, baking soda, cinnamon, and nutmeg.
2. In another bowl, mix the pumpkin puree, sugar, eggs, and vegetable oil.
3. Combine the wet and dry ingredients until just mixed.
4. Divide the batter evenly between 12 muffin cases in an air fryer-safe muffin tin.
5. Preheat the air fryer to 160°C (320°F) and cook for 16-18 minutes, until a toothpick inserted in the centre comes out clean.
6. Let the muffins cool on a wire rack before serving.

Nutritional Info: Calories: 180 | Fat: 8g | Carbs: 25g | Protein: 3g

SESAME BAGELS

Prep: 15 mins | Cook: 15 mins | Serves: 6 bagels

Ingredients:

- **UK:** 300g gluten-free flour, 10g instant yeast, 1 tablespoon sugar, 1 teaspoon salt, 150ml warm water, 2 tablespoons sesame seeds

Instructions:

1. In a bowl, combine the gluten-free flour, yeast, sugar, and salt.
2. Gradually add the warm water and knead into a smooth dough.
3. Divide the dough into 6 equal pieces and shape into bagels by forming rounds and poking a hole in the centre.
4. Preheat the air fryer to 180°C (350°F) and brush the tops of the bagels with a little water. Sprinkle sesame seeds on top.
5. Place the bagels in the air fryer basket and bake for 12-15 minutes until golden and firm.
6. Let them cool slightly before serving with your favourite spreads.

Nutritional Info: Calories: 220 | Fat: 4g | Carbs: 38g | Protein: 5g

CHOCOLATE CHIP COOKIES

Prep: 10 mins | Cook: 10 mins | Serves: 12 cookies

Ingredients:

- **UK:** 150g gluten-free flour, 100g unsalted butter (softened), 100g sugar, 50g brown sugar, 1 egg, 1/2 teaspoon baking soda, 100g dark chocolate chips

Instructions:

1. Cream together the softened butter, sugar, and brown sugar until light and fluffy.
2. Beat in the egg until fully combined.
3. Stir in the flour and baking soda, then fold in the chocolate chips.
4. Scoop the dough into 12 balls and place them on parchment paper in the air fryer basket.
5. Preheat the air fryer to 170°C (340°F) and cook for 8-10 minutes until the cookies are golden around the edges but still soft in the centre.
6. Allow the cookies to cool slightly before enjoying their gooey centres.

Nutritional Info: Calories: 180 | Fat: 9g | Carbs: 24g | Protein: 2g

HERB-CRUSTED ROAST CHICKEN

Prep: 10 mins | Cook: 50 mins | Serves: 4

Ingredients:

- **UK:** 1 whole chicken (about 1.5kg), 30ml olive oil, 1 tablespoon dried mixed herbs, 1 teaspoon garlic powder, 1 teaspoon onion powder, salt, pepper, lemon wedges (for serving)

Instructions:

1. Preheat your air fryer to 180°C (350°F). Use the roast setting if your air fryer has this function.
2. Pat the chicken dry with kitchen paper and rub it all over with olive oil.
3. In a small bowl, mix the dried herbs, garlic powder, onion powder, salt, and pepper. Rub this seasoning mix all over the chicken, making sure it's well-coated.
4. Place the chicken breast-side down in the air fryer basket.
5. Cook for 25 minutes, then carefully flip the chicken using tongs. Cook for an additional 25 minutes, or until the internal temperature reaches 75°C (165°F) at the thickest part.
6. Let the chicken rest for 10 minutes before carving. Serve with lemon wedges for a burst of freshness.

Nutritional Info: Calories: 420 | Fat: 28g | Carbs: 2g | Protein: 37g

GLUTEN-FREE FISH AND CHIPS

Prep: 15 mins | Cook: 20 mins | Serves: 4

Ingredients:

- **UK:** 500g cod fillets, 100g gluten-free breadcrumbs, 2 eggs (beaten), 2 tablespoons gluten-free flour, 500g potatoes (peeled and cut into chips), 30ml olive oil, salt, pepper, lemon wedges

Instructions:

1. Preheat your air fryer to 200°C (400°F).
2. Toss the potato chips in olive oil, salt, and pepper. Arrange them in the air fryer basket in a single layer and cook for 15-20 minutes, shaking halfway through until golden and crispy.
3. While the chips cook, pat the cod fillets dry. Dredge them in gluten-free flour, dip in the beaten egg, and then coat in gluten-free breadcrumbs.
4. Once the chips are done, remove them from the air fryer and keep them warm. Lower the temperature to 180°C (350°F).
5. Place the breaded fish in the air fryer and cook for 10-12 minutes, flipping halfway, until golden and cooked through.
6. Serve the fish and chips hot with lemon wedges and a side of tartar sauce.

Nutritional Info: Calories: 450 | Fat: 12g | Carbs: 60g | Protein: 25g

STUFFED BELL PEPPERS WITH QUINOA AND BLACK BEANS

Prep: 15 mins | Cook: 25 mins | Serves: 4

Ingredients:

- **UK:** 4 large bell peppers (tops removed, seeds scooped), 150g cooked quinoa, 200g black beans (drained), 100g grated cheese (optional), 1 tablespoon olive oil, 1 teaspoon cumin, salt, pepper, fresh coriander (for garnish)

Instructions:

1. Preheat your air fryer to 180°C (350°F).
2. In a bowl, mix the cooked quinoa, black beans, olive oil, cumin, salt, and pepper. Stir in the cheese, if using.
3. Stuff each bell pepper with the quinoa mixture and place them upright in the air fryer basket.
4. Cook for 20-25 minutes, or until the peppers are tender and slightly charred on top.
5. Garnish with fresh coriander and serve immediately.

Nutritional Info: Calories: 280 | Fat: 10g | Carbs: 38g | Protein: 12g

LEMON AND GARLIC SALMON FILLETS

Prep: 5 mins | Cook: 10 mins | Serves: 2

Ingredients:

- **UK:** 2 salmon fillets (about 150g each), 1 tablespoon olive oil, 1 garlic clove (minced), 1 tablespoon lemon juice, salt, pepper, lemon slices (for garnish)

Instructions:

1. Preheat your air fryer to 200°C (400°F).
2. Rub the salmon fillets with olive oil, minced garlic, lemon juice, salt, and pepper.
3. Place the fillets skin-side down in the air fryer basket and cook for 8-10 minutes until the salmon is flaky and cooked through.
4. Garnish with lemon slices and serve with your favourite sides.

Nutritional Info: Calories: 280 | Fat: 18g | Carbs: 1g | Protein: 25g

CRISPY PORK BELLY WITH APPLE SAUCE

Prep: 15 mins | Cook: 40 mins | Serves: 4

Ingredients:

- **UK:** 600g pork belly (skin scored), 1 tablespoon olive oil, 1 teaspoon sea salt, 2 apples (peeled and chopped), 1 tablespoon honey, 1 teaspoon cinnamon

Instructions:

1. Preheat your air fryer to 200°C (400°F).
2. Rub the pork belly with olive oil and sea salt, making sure to get the salt into the scored skin.
3. Place the pork belly in the air fryer, skin-side up, and cook for 30-40 minutes until the skin is crispy and golden.
4. Meanwhile, make the apple sauce by simmering the apples, honey, and cinnamon in a small saucepan until the apples break down and form a sauce.
5. Slice the pork belly and serve with the warm apple sauce.

Nutritional Info: Calories: 560 | Fat: 45g | Carbs: 15g | Protein: 28g

VEGETABLE AND CHICKPEA CURRY

Prep: 15 mins | Cook: 20 mins | Serves: 4

Ingredients:

- **UK:** 1 tablespoon olive oil, 1 onion (chopped), 2 garlic cloves (minced), 1 tablespoon curry powder, 1 teaspoon ground cumin, 1 teaspoon ground coriander, 400g tin chopped tomatoes, 400g tin chickpeas (drained and rinsed), 200g baby spinach, 200ml coconut milk, salt, pepper, fresh coriander (for garnish)

Instructions:

1. Preheat your air fryer to 180°C (350°F).
2. In a large frying pan, heat the olive oil and sauté the onion and garlic for 3-4 minutes until softened.
3. Stir in the curry powder, ground cumin, and ground coriander, and cook for another minute.
4. Add the chopped tomatoes, chickpeas, and coconut milk. Stir well and season with salt and pepper.
5. Transfer the curry mixture to an air fryer-safe dish and cook in the air fryer for 15-20 minutes, stirring occasionally.
6. Stir in the baby spinach in the last 5 minutes of cooking, allowing it to wilt.
7. Garnish with fresh coriander and serve with rice or gluten-free naan bread.

Nutritional Info: Calories: 310 | Fat: 14g | Carbs: 36g | Protein: 9g

GLUTEN-FREE CHICKEN KIEV

Prep: 20 mins | Cook: 18 mins | Serves: 4

Ingredients:

- **UK:** 4 chicken breasts (about 150g each), 100g gluten-free breadcrumbs, 2 eggs (beaten), 100g butter (softened), 2 garlic cloves (minced), 1 tablespoon chopped parsley, 2 tablespoons gluten-free flour, salt, pepper

Instructions:

1. Preheat your air fryer to 180°C (350°F).
2. In a small bowl, mix the softened butter, minced garlic, and chopped parsley. Shape the mixture into small logs and freeze for 10 minutes.
3. Butterfly the chicken breasts by slicing them horizontally, making a pocket. Insert a butter log into each breast.
4. Dredge the stuffed chicken in gluten-free flour, dip in the beaten eggs, and coat in gluten-free breadcrumbs.
5. Place the chicken in the air fryer basket and cook for 15-18 minutes, turning halfway through, until golden and cooked through.
6. Serve the Chicken Kiev hot with a side salad or steamed vegetables.

Nutritional Info: Calories: 520 | Fat: 30g | Carbs: 25g | Protein: 40g

STUFFED PORTOBELLO MUSHROOMS

Prep: 10 mins | Cook: 12 mins | Serves: 4

Ingredients:

- **UK:** 4 large Portobello mushrooms (stems removed), 200g ricotta cheese, 50g grated Parmesan cheese, 1 garlic clove (minced), 1 tablespoon olive oil, salt, pepper, fresh basil (for garnish)

Instructions:

1. Preheat your air fryer to 180°C (350°F).
2. In a bowl, mix the ricotta cheese, Parmesan, minced garlic, salt, and pepper.
3. Brush the Portobello mushrooms with olive oil and stuff each with the ricotta mixture.
4. Place the stuffed mushrooms in the air fryer basket and cook for 10-12 minutes until the mushrooms are tender and the filling is golden on top.
5. Garnish with fresh basil and serve as a main or side dish.

Nutritional Info: Calories: 230 | Fat: 16g | Carbs: 7g | Protein: 13g

HONEY AND MUSTARD GLAZED GAMMON

Prep: 10 mins | Cook: 25 mins | Serves: 4

Ingredients:

- **UK:** 600g gammon joint, 2 tablespoons honey, 2 tablespoons Dijon mustard, 1 tablespoon olive oil, 1 teaspoon black pepper, fresh thyme (for garnish)

Instructions:

1. Preheat your air fryer to 180°C (350°F).
2. In a small bowl, mix the honey, Dijon mustard, olive oil, and black pepper.
3. Brush the gammon joint with the honey mustard glaze, making sure it's fully coated.
4. Place the gammon in the air fryer and cook for 20-25 minutes, flipping halfway, until the gammon is caramelised and cooked through.
5. Garnish with fresh thyme and serve with roasted vegetables or mashed potatoes.

Nutritional Info: Calories: 380 | Fat: 15g | Carbs: 15g | Protein: 45g

CRISPY TOFU STIR-FRY

Prep: 15 mins | Cook: 15 mins | Serves: 4

Ingredients:

- **UK:** 400g firm tofu (pressed and cubed), 2 tablespoons gluten-free soy sauce, 1 tablespoon sesame oil, 1 tablespoon olive oil, 1 red bell pepper (sliced), 1 courgette (sliced), 1 carrot (julienned), 100g snap peas, 1 teaspoon ginger (minced), 1 garlic clove (minced), 1 tablespoon sesame seeds (for garnish)

Instructions:

1. Preheat your air fryer to 200°C (400°F).
2. Toss the cubed tofu in 1 tablespoon of gluten-free soy sauce and sesame oil.
3. Place the tofu in the air fryer basket and cook for 12-15 minutes, shaking halfway, until crispy and golden.
4. While the tofu cooks, heat olive oil in a frying pan and sauté the garlic, ginger, bell pepper, courgette, carrot, and snap peas for 4-5 minutes until tender.
5. Once the tofu is ready, toss it with the stir-fried vegetables and the remaining soy sauce.
6. Garnish with sesame seeds and serve hot.

Nutritional Info: Calories: 320 | Fat: 18g | Carbs: 15g | Protein: 20g

LEMON GARLIC CHICKEN DRUMSTICKS

Prep: 10 mins | Cook: 25 mins | Serves: 4

Ingredients:

- **UK:** 8 chicken drumsticks, 30ml olive oil, 2 tablespoons lemon juice, 2 garlic cloves (minced), 1 teaspoon dried oregano, salt, pepper, lemon wedges (for garnish)

Instructions:

1. Preheat your air fryer to 200°C (390°F) for 5 minutes.
2. In a bowl, combine olive oil, lemon juice, minced garlic, oregano, salt, and pepper. Toss the chicken drumsticks in the mixture until well coated.
3. Arrange the drumsticks in a single layer in the air fryer basket, ensuring they aren't overcrowded for even cooking.
4. Set the air fryer to 200°C (390°F) and cook for 25 minutes, flipping the drumsticks halfway through using tongs for even browning.
5. Once the chicken is crispy and cooked through (internal temperature should reach 74°C/165°F), remove from the air fryer.
6. Garnish with lemon wedges and serve hot.

Nutritional Info: Calories: 320 | Fat: 22g | Carbs: 2g | Protein: 28g

HONEY MUSTARD CHICKEN THIGHS

Prep: 10 mins | Cook: 20 mins | Serves: 4

Ingredients:

- **UK:** 4 boneless, skinless chicken thighs, 2 tablespoons honey, 1 tablespoon Dijon mustard, 1 tablespoon wholegrain mustard, 15ml olive oil, 1 teaspoon garlic powder, salt, pepper

Instructions:

1. Preheat your air fryer to 180°C (355°F) for 3-4 minutes.
2. In a small bowl, whisk together honey, Dijon mustard, wholegrain mustard, olive oil, garlic powder, salt, and pepper.
3. Rub the mixture all over the chicken thighs until they are evenly coated.
4. Place the chicken thighs in the air fryer basket in a single layer.
5. Air fry at 180°C (355°F) for 18-20 minutes, turning halfway through to ensure even cooking. The chicken should be golden and caramelised.
6. Once the chicken reaches an internal temperature of 74°C (165°F), remove and let rest for a couple of minutes before serving.

Nutritional Info: Calories: 290 | Fat: 14g | Carbs: 10g | Protein: 30g

CAJUN CHICKEN TENDERS

Prep: 10 mins | Cook: 12 mins | Serves: 4

Ingredients:

- **UK:** 500g chicken tenders, 1 tablespoon Cajun seasoning, 1 tablespoon olive oil, 60g gluten-free breadcrumbs, 30g grated Parmesan, salt, pepper, 1 egg (beaten)

Instructions:

1. Preheat the air fryer to 200°C (390°F) for 5 minutes.
2. In a shallow dish, mix gluten-free breadcrumbs, grated Parmesan, Cajun seasoning, salt, and pepper.
3. Dip each chicken tender into the beaten egg, then coat in the breadcrumb mixture, pressing firmly to help it stick.
4. Lightly spray or brush the air fryer basket with olive oil to prevent sticking.
5. Arrange the chicken tenders in the basket, leaving space between each one.
6. Air fry at 200°C (390°F) for 10-12 minutes, flipping halfway through. The tenders should be golden and crispy when done.
7. Serve with your favourite dipping sauce or a side salad.

Nutritional Info: Calories: 350 | Fat: 15g | Carbs: 12g | Protein: 40g

BBQ CHICKEN WINGS

Prep: 5 mins | Cook: 20 mins | Serves: 4

Ingredients:

- **UK:** 12 chicken wings, 60ml gluten-free BBQ sauce, 1 tablespoon olive oil, salt, pepper, 1 teaspoon smoked paprika

Instructions:

1. Preheat your air fryer to 200°C (390°F) for 5 minutes.
2. Toss the chicken wings in olive oil, salt, pepper, and smoked paprika until evenly coated.
3. Arrange the wings in the air fryer basket in a single layer.
4. Cook at 200°C (390°F) for 15 minutes, shaking the basket halfway through to ensure even crisping.
5. After 15 minutes, brush the wings with gluten-free BBQ sauce and cook for an additional 5 minutes to allow the sauce to caramelise.
6. Serve hot with extra BBQ sauce on the side.

Nutritional Info: Calories: 380 | Fat: 22g | Carbs: 6g | Protein: 30g

CRISPY CHICKEN BREAST WITH HERBS

Prep: 10 mins | Cook: 12 mins | Serves: 2

Ingredients:

- **UK:** 2 boneless, skinless chicken breasts, 1 tablespoon olive oil, 1 teaspoon dried thyme, 1 teaspoon dried rosemary, 1 teaspoon garlic powder, salt, pepper

Instructions:

1. Preheat your air fryer to 190°C (375°F) for 3-4 minutes.
2. In a small bowl, mix olive oil, thyme, rosemary, garlic powder, salt, and pepper.
3. Rub the herb mixture evenly over both sides of the chicken breasts.
4. Place the chicken breasts in the air fryer basket, ensuring they are not overlapping.
5. Air fry at 190°C (375°F) for 10-12 minutes, turning halfway through. The chicken should be golden on the outside and fully cooked through (internal temperature of 74°C/165°F).
6. Let the chicken rest for a few minutes before serving.

Nutritional Info: Calories: 250 | Fat: 10g | Carbs: 1g | Protein: 38g

GARLIC PARMESAN CHICKEN NUGGETS

Prep: 10 mins | Cook: 10 mins | Serves: 4

Ingredients:

- **UK:** 500g chicken breast (cut into bite-sized pieces), 50g gluten-free breadcrumbs, 30g grated Parmesan, 1 teaspoon garlic powder, 1 tablespoon olive oil, 1 egg (beaten), salt, pepper

Instructions:

1. Preheat your air fryer to 200°C (390°F) for 5 minutes.
2. In a shallow dish, mix breadcrumbs, grated Parmesan, garlic powder, salt, and pepper.
3. Dip each chicken nugget into the beaten egg, then coat in the breadcrumb mixture.
4. Lightly oil the air fryer basket and arrange the chicken nuggets in a single layer.
5. Air fry at 200°C (390°F) for 8-10 minutes, shaking the basket halfway through to ensure even cooking. The nuggets should be golden and crispy.
6. Serve with a garlic aioli or marinara sauce for dipping.

Nutritional Info: Calories: 310 | Fat: 14g | Carbs: 8g | Protein: 38g

TERIYAKI CHICKEN SKEWERS

Prep: 15 mins | Cook: 10 mins | Serves: 4

Ingredients:

- **UK:** 500g chicken breast (cut into cubes), 60ml gluten-free teriyaki sauce, 1 tablespoon sesame oil, 1 red pepper (cut into cubes), 1 courgette (cut into slices), wooden skewers (soaked in water for 30 minutes)

Instructions:

1. Preheat your air fryer to 190°C (375°F) for 3-4 minutes.
2. Thread the chicken, red pepper, and courgette onto the skewers.
3. Brush the skewers with sesame oil and season with salt and pepper.
4. Place the skewers in the air fryer basket and cook at 190°C (375°F) for 8-10 minutes, flipping halfway through.
5. Once cooked through, brush the skewers with gluten-free teriyaki sauce and cook for an additional 2 minutes.
6. Serve with a side of rice or salad.

Nutritional Info: Calories: 280 | Fat: 12g | Carbs: 10g | Protein: 32g

ROSEMARY ROAST TURKEY BREAST

Prep: 5 mins | Cook: 25 mins | Serves: 4

Ingredients:

- **UK:** 500g turkey breast, 2 tablespoons olive oil, 1 tablespoon fresh rosemary (chopped), 2 garlic cloves (minced), salt, pepper

Instructions:

1. Preheat the air fryer to 180°C (355°F) for 5 minutes.
2. Rub the turkey breast with olive oil, minced garlic, rosemary, salt, and pepper.
3. Place the turkey breast in the air fryer basket, skin side up if applicable.
4. Cook at 180°C (355°F) for 20-25 minutes, turning halfway through. The turkey should be golden and fully cooked (internal temperature of 74°C/165°F).
5. Let the turkey rest for 5 minutes before slicing and serving.

Nutritional Info: Calories: 220 | Fat: 8g | Carbs: 0g | Protein: 36g

GREEK LEMON CHICKEN SOUVLAKI

Prep: 15 mins | Cook: 10 mins | Serves: 4

Ingredients:

- **UK:** 500g chicken breast (cut into cubes), 2 tablespoons lemon juice, 2 tablespoons olive oil, 1 teaspoon dried oregano, 2 garlic cloves (minced), salt, pepper, wooden skewers (soaked in water for 30 minutes)

Instructions:

1. Preheat your air fryer to 190°C (375°F) for 5 minutes.
2. In a bowl, mix lemon juice, olive oil, oregano, garlic, salt, and pepper.
3. Toss the chicken cubes in the marinade and thread them onto the soaked skewers.
4. Place the skewers in the air fryer basket and cook at 190°C (375°F) for 8-10 minutes, flipping halfway through.
5. Serve with gluten-free pita bread, tzatziki, and a side of salad.

Nutritional Info: Calories: 280 | Fat: 12g | Carbs: 2g | Protein: 36g

BUFFALO CHICKEN TENDERS

Prep: 10 mins | Cook: 12 mins | Serves: 4

Ingredients:

- **UK:** 500g chicken tenders, 60ml gluten-free hot sauce, 1 tablespoon olive oil, 30g gluten-free breadcrumbs, 1 teaspoon garlic powder, salt, pepper

Instructions:

1. Preheat your air fryer to 200°C (390°F) for 5 minutes.
2. Toss the chicken tenders with olive oil, garlic powder, salt, and pepper.
3. Dip the tenders into gluten-free breadcrumbs to coat.
4. Arrange the tenders in the air fryer basket in a single layer.
5. Air fry at 200°C (390°F) for 10-12 minutes, turning halfway through. The tenders should be crispy and golden.
6. Once cooked, toss the tenders in gluten-free hot sauce and serve immediately.

Nutritional Info: Calories: 320 | Fat: 14g | Carbs: 6g | Protein: 42g

CRISPY ROAST POTATOES

Prep: 10 mins | Cook: 25 mins | Serves: 4

Ingredients:

- **UK:** 600g potatoes (peeled and chopped into 2cm cubes), 2 tablespoons olive oil, 1 teaspoon garlic powder, 1 teaspoon paprika, salt, pepper, fresh rosemary (optional)

Instructions:

1. Preheat your air fryer to 200°C (392°F).
2. In a large bowl, toss the potato cubes with olive oil, garlic powder, paprika, salt, and pepper until evenly coated.
3. Spread the potatoes in a single layer in the air fryer basket. Use the 'roast' function and cook for 20-25 minutes, shaking halfway through.
4. For extra crispiness, increase the temperature to 220°C (428°F) for the last 5 minutes.
5. Once golden and crispy, remove the potatoes from the air fryer. Garnish with fresh rosemary if using.

Nutritional Info: Calories: 180 | Fat: 7g | Carbs: 28g | Protein: 3g

GARLIC AND PARMESAN COURGETTE FRIES

Prep: 10 mins | Cook: 12 mins | Serves: 4

Ingredients:

- **UK:** 3 medium courgettes (cut into sticks), 50g gluten-free breadcrumbs, 30g grated Parmesan, 1 teaspoon garlic powder, 1 large egg, salt, pepper

Instructions:

1. Preheat your air fryer to 190°C (374°F).
2. In a bowl, mix the breadcrumbs, Parmesan, garlic powder, salt, and pepper.
3. Beat the egg in a separate bowl, then dip each courgette stick into the egg, followed by the breadcrumb mixture.
4. Place the courgette fries in the air fryer basket in a single layer, using the 'air fry' function. Cook for 10-12 minutes, shaking halfway through, until crispy and golden.
5. Serve immediately for the perfect crunchy side.

Nutritional Info: Calories: 120 | Fat: 6g | Carbs: 10g | Protein: 7g

HONEY-GLAZED CARROTS

Prep: 5 mins | Cook: 15 mins | Serves: 4

Ingredients:

- **UK:** 500g carrots (peeled and sliced into sticks), 30ml olive oil, 2 tablespoons honey, salt, pepper, fresh parsley (for garnish)

Instructions:

1. Preheat the air fryer to 180°C (356°F).
2. Toss the carrot sticks in olive oil, honey, salt, and pepper until evenly coated.
3. Place the carrots in the air fryer basket and use the 'roast' function for 12-15 minutes, shaking halfway through.
4. Once tender and slightly caramelised, remove from the air fryer and garnish with fresh parsley.

Nutritional Info: Calories: 110 | Fat: 5g | Carbs: 15g | Protein: 1g

CRISPY BRUSSELS SPROUTS WITH BALSAMIC GLAZE

Prep: 5 mins | Cook: 15 mins | Serves: 4

Ingredients:

- **UK:** 400g Brussels sprouts (halved), 2 tablespoons olive oil, salt, pepper, 2 tablespoons balsamic glaze

Instructions:

1. Preheat your air fryer to 200°C (392°F).
2. Toss the Brussels sprouts in olive oil, salt, and pepper.
3. Use the 'air fry' function to cook the sprouts for 12-15 minutes, shaking halfway through, until crispy and browned on the edges.
4. Drizzle with balsamic glaze before serving.

Nutritional Info: Calories: 120 | Fat: 7g | Carbs: 12g | Protein: 3g

SWEET POTATO WEDGES

Prep: 5 mins | Cook: 20 mins | Serves: 4

Ingredients:

- **UK:** 500g sweet potatoes (cut into wedges), 2 tablespoons olive oil, 1 teaspoon paprika, salt, pepper

Instructions:

1. Preheat the air fryer to 200°C (392°F).
2. Toss the sweet potato wedges in olive oil, paprika, salt, and pepper.
3. Place the wedges in a single layer in the air fryer basket. Use the 'air fry' function and cook for 18-20 minutes, flipping halfway through, until crispy on the outside and tender on the inside.
4. Serve hot as a tasty side or snack.

Nutritional Info: Calories: 160 | Fat: 6g | Carbs: 27g | Protein: 2g

CAULIFLOWER 'WINGS' WITH BUFFALO SAUCE

Prep: 10 mins | Cook: 20 mins | Serves: 4

Ingredients:

- **UK:** 1 medium cauliflower (cut into florets), 60g gluten-free flour, 120ml almond milk, 1 teaspoon garlic powder, 1 teaspoon paprika, 2 tablespoons buffalo sauce

Instructions:

1. Preheat your air fryer to 190°C (374°F).
2. Mix the flour, almond milk, garlic powder, and paprika into a batter. Dip the cauliflower florets into the batter, ensuring they're well coated.
3. Use the 'air fry' function to cook the florets for 18-20 minutes, shaking halfway through.
4. Once crispy, toss the florets in buffalo sauce and return to the air fryer for an additional 2-3 minutes.
5. Serve hot with a dipping sauce of your choice.

Nutritional Info: Calories: 150 | Fat: 3g | Carbs: 26g | Protein: 5g

HERBED GREEN BEANS

Prep: 5 mins | Cook: 10 mins | Serves: 4

Ingredients:

- **UK:** 400g green beans (trimmed), 1 tablespoon olive oil, 1 teaspoon dried herbs (thyme, oregano, or rosemary), salt, pepper

Instructions:

1. Preheat the air fryer to 190°C (374°F).
2. Toss the green beans with olive oil, herbs, salt, and pepper.
3. Use the 'air fry' function to cook the beans for 8-10 minutes, shaking halfway through, until tender and lightly crisped.
4. Serve immediately as a fresh, herby side.

Nutritional Info: Calories: 80 | Fat: 5g | Carbs: 7g | Protein: 2g

CRISPY POLENTA CHIPS

Prep: 10 mins | Cook: 15 mins | Serves: 4

Ingredients:

- **UK:** 500g pre-cooked polenta (cut into chips), 2 tablespoons olive oil, 1 teaspoon garlic powder, salt, pepper, grated Parmesan (optional)

Instructions:

1. Preheat your air fryer to 200°C (392°F).
2. Toss the polenta chips in olive oil, garlic powder, salt, and pepper.
3. Place in the air fryer basket, using the 'air fry' function, and cook for 12-15 minutes, shaking halfway through, until crispy.
4. Optionally sprinkle with grated Parmesan before serving.

Nutritional Info: Calories: 150 | Fat: 7g | Carbs: 20g | Protein: 3g

ROASTED MEDITERRANEAN VEGETABLES

Prep: 5 mins | Cook: 15 mins | Serves: 4

Ingredients:

- **UK:** 1 aubergine (chopped), 1 red pepper (chopped), 1 courgette (sliced), 1 red onion (chopped), 2 tablespoons olive oil, 1 teaspoon dried oregano, salt, pepper

Instructions:

1. Preheat the air fryer to 190°C (374°F).
2. Toss the chopped vegetables with olive oil, oregano, salt, and pepper.
3. Use the 'roast' function to cook for 12-15 minutes, shaking halfway through, until tender and slightly charred.
4. Serve as a colourful, nutritious side.

Nutritional Info: Calories: 100 | Fat: 6g | Carbs: 10g | Protein: 2g

CHEESY CAULIFLOWER BITES

Prep: 10 mins | Cook: 15 mins | Serves: 4

Ingredients:

- **UK:** 1 medium cauliflower (cut into florets), 60g gluten-free breadcrumbs, 50g grated cheddar cheese, 1 large egg, salt, pepper

Instructions:

1. Preheat your air fryer to 190°C (374°F).
2. In a bowl, mix the breadcrumbs, cheese, salt, and pepper.
3. Dip each cauliflower floret in the beaten egg, then coat with the breadcrumb mixture.
4. Use the 'air fry' function and cook for 12-15 minutes, shaking halfway through, until golden and crispy.
5. Serve hot with your favourite dipping sauce.

Nutritional Info: Calories: 130 | Fat: 6g | Carbs: 14g | Protein: 6g

BEEF WELLINGTON BITES

Prep: 15 mins | Cook: 12 mins | Serves: 4

Ingredients:

- **UK:** 450g beef fillet, 200g gluten-free puff pastry, 150g mushrooms (finely chopped), 1 tablespoon Dijon mustard, 1 egg (beaten), salt, pepper, olive oil spray

Instructions:

1. Preheat your air fryer to 200°C (392°F).
2. Season the beef fillet with salt and pepper, then sear it in a hot pan over medium heat for about 2-3 minutes on each side. Let it cool slightly before spreading a thin layer of Dijon mustard on all sides.
3. Sauté the mushrooms in a pan until softened and moisture has evaporated. Let them cool.
4. Roll out the gluten-free puff pastry and spread the mushrooms over the centre. Place the beef on top and wrap the pastry around it, sealing the edges tightly.
5. Brush the pastry with beaten egg and cut it into bite-sized portions.
6. Lightly spray your air fryer basket with olive oil, place the bites inside, and air fry for 10-12 minutes until golden brown.
7. Serve hot with a side of gluten-free gravy.

Nutritional Info: Calories: 320 | Fat: 18g | Carbs: 22g | Protein: 20g

LOBSTER TAILS WITH GARLIC BUTTER

Prep: 10 mins | Cook: 10 mins | Serves: 2

Ingredients:

- **UK:** 2 lobster tails (about 200g each), 4 tablespoons unsalted butter, 2 garlic cloves (minced), 1 tablespoon lemon juice, 1 teaspoon parsley (chopped), salt, pepper

Instructions:

1. Preheat your air fryer to 190°C (375°F).
2. Using kitchen shears, cut the top shell of the lobster tails lengthwise and pull the meat out, laying it on top of the shell.
3. Melt the butter in a small pan and mix in the garlic, lemon juice, salt, and pepper. Brush this garlic butter generously over the lobster meat.
4. Place the lobster tails in the air fryer basket, meat-side up.
5. Air fry for 8-10 minutes, until the lobster is opaque and cooked through. The internal temperature should reach 60°C (140°F).
6. Garnish with fresh parsley and serve with extra garlic butter for dipping.

Nutritional Info: Calories: 280 | Fat: 19g | Carbs: 2g | Protein: 24g

STUFFED CORNISH HENS

Prep: 20 mins | Cook: 30 mins | Serves: 4

Ingredients:

- **UK:** 2 Cornish hens (500g each), 100g gluten-free bread (cubed), 50g dried cranberries, 50g pecans (chopped), 1 small onion (chopped), 2 tablespoons olive oil, 1 teaspoon thyme, 1 teaspoon rosemary, salt, pepper

Instructions:

1. Preheat your air fryer to 180°C (356°F).
2. In a pan, heat the olive oil over medium heat and sauté the onion until soft. Add the cranberries, pecans, thyme, rosemary, salt, and pepper, stirring for a few minutes. Toss the gluten-free bread cubes into the mixture to create the stuffing.
3. Stuff each Cornish hen with the prepared mixture and tie the legs together using kitchen string.
4. Rub the hens with olive oil and season the skin with salt and pepper.
5. Place the hens in the air fryer basket and cook for 25-30 minutes, turning halfway through. Ensure the internal temperature reaches 75°C (165°F).
6. Let the hens rest for 5 minutes before serving.

Nutritional Info: Calories: 450 | Fat: 25g | Carbs: 18g | Protein: 35g

MUSHROOM RISOTTO BALLS

Prep: 15 mins | Cook: 15 mins | Serves: 4

Ingredients:

- **UK:** 200g Arborio rice, 500ml gluten-free vegetable stock, 100g mushrooms (finely chopped), 1 small onion (finely chopped), 2 tablespoons olive oil, 50g Parmesan cheese (grated), 1 egg (beaten), 100g gluten-free breadcrumbs, salt, pepper

Instructions:

1. In a pan, heat the olive oil over medium heat. Add the onion and mushrooms, sautéing until softened.
2. Stir in the Arborio rice, toasting it for 2 minutes, then gradually add the vegetable stock, stirring frequently until the rice is al dente (about 18 minutes).
3. Once cooked, stir in the grated Parmesan cheese, salt, and pepper. Let the risotto cool slightly.
4. Once cooled, form small balls with the risotto mixture, dip them in beaten egg, and coat with gluten-free breadcrumbs.
5. Preheat your air fryer to 200°C (392°F).
6. Lightly spray the basket with olive oil and arrange the risotto balls in a single layer. Air fry for 10-12 minutes until golden and crispy.
7. Serve warm with a side of marinara sauce for dipping.

Nutritional Info: Calories: 300 | Fat: 10g | Carbs: 42g | Protein: 8g

RACK OF LAMB WITH HERB CRUST

Prep: 20 mins | Cook: 25 mins | Serves: 4

Ingredients:

- **UK:** 1 rack of lamb (about 800g), 100g gluten-free breadcrumbs, 2 tablespoons Dijon mustard, 2 garlic cloves (minced), 2 tablespoons fresh rosemary (chopped), 2 tablespoons fresh thyme (chopped), salt, pepper

Instructions:

1. Preheat your air fryer to 200°C (392°F).
2. Season the rack of lamb with salt and pepper. In a small bowl, mix the breadcrumbs, garlic, rosemary, and thyme.
3. Brush the lamb with Dijon mustard and press the breadcrumb mixture onto the meat, ensuring it's well coated.
4. Place the lamb in the air fryer basket and cook for 20-25 minutes, or until it reaches an internal temperature of 60°C (140°F) for medium-rare.
5. Let the lamb rest for 5 minutes before slicing into chops. Serve with seasonal vegetables.

Nutritional Info: Calories: 400 | Fat: 30g | Carbs: 10g | Protein: 30g

SEAFOOD PAELLA

Prep: 15 mins | Cook: 25 mins | Serves: 4

Ingredients:

- **UK:** 200g Arborio rice, 500ml gluten-free chicken stock, 150g prawns (peeled), 150g mussels (cleaned), 100g squid (sliced), 1 small onion (chopped), 1 bell pepper (chopped), 2 garlic cloves (minced), 1 teaspoon paprika, 1 tablespoon olive oil, salt, pepper, lemon wedges (for serving)

Instructions:

1. Preheat your air fryer to 190°C (375°F).
2. In a pan, heat the olive oil over medium heat. Sauté the onion, bell pepper, and garlic until softened.
3. Stir in the Arborio rice and paprika, cooking for another minute before adding the chicken stock.
4. Pour the mixture into the air fryer basket and add the prawns, mussels, and squid.
5. Air fry for 20-25 minutes, stirring halfway through, until the seafood is cooked and the rice is tender.
6. Serve with lemon wedges for a zesty touch.

Nutritional Info: Calories: 350 | Fat: 8g | Carbs: 50g | Protein: 20g

CAPRESE STUFFED PORTOBELLO MUSHROOMS

Prep: 10 mins | Cook: 12 mins | Serves: 4

Ingredients:

- **UK:** 4 large Portobello mushrooms, 200g cherry tomatoes (halved), 150g mozzarella cheese (cubed), 2 tablespoons balsamic glaze, 1 tablespoon olive oil, salt, pepper, fresh basil leaves (for garnish)

Instructions:

1. Preheat your air fryer to 200°C (392°F).
2. Clean the Portobello mushrooms and remove the stems. Brush them with olive oil and season with salt and pepper.
3. In a bowl, mix the cherry tomatoes and mozzarella cheese, then spoon this mixture into the mushroom caps.
4. Drizzle balsamic glaze over the stuffed mushrooms.
5. Place the mushrooms in the air fryer basket and cook for 10-12 minutes until the cheese is melted and bubbly.
6. Garnish with fresh basil leaves before serving.

Nutritional Info: Calories: 220 | Fat: 14g | Carbs: 10g | Protein: 12g

BEEF TENDERLOIN WITH RED WINE SAUCE

Prep: 15 mins | Cook: 20 mins | Serves: 2

Ingredients:

- **UK:** 400g beef tenderloin, 150ml red wine, 2 tablespoons butter, 1 small shallot (finely chopped), salt, pepper, olive oil spray

Instructions:

1. Preheat your air fryer to 200°C (392°F).
2. Season the beef tenderloin with salt and pepper. Lightly spray the air fryer basket with olive oil and place the tenderloin inside.
3. Cook for 15-20 minutes, or until the internal temperature reaches your desired doneness (medium-rare is 55°C/130°F).
4. Meanwhile, in a small saucepan, melt the butter and sauté the shallot until soft. Add the red wine and simmer until reduced by half.
5. Once the tenderloin is done, let it rest for 5 minutes before slicing. Serve with the red wine sauce drizzled over.

Nutritional Info: Calories: 480 | Fat: 25g | Carbs: 5g | Protein: 60g

CHICKEN CORDON BLEU

Prep: 15 mins | Cook: 20 mins | Serves: 4

Ingredients:

- **UK:** 4 chicken breasts (about 150g each), 100g ham slices, 100g gluten-free cheese (sliced), 1 egg (beaten), 100g gluten-free breadcrumbs, salt, pepper, olive oil spray

Instructions:

1. Preheat your air fryer to 200°C (392°F).
2. Place a chicken breast between two sheets of cling film and pound it to about 1cm thick. Season with salt and pepper.
3. Layer a slice of ham and cheese on top of the chicken, then roll it tightly and secure with toothpicks.
4. Dip each roll in beaten egg, then coat with gluten-free breadcrumbs.
5. Lightly spray the air fryer basket with olive oil and arrange the chicken rolls inside.
6. Cook for 18-20 minutes until golden brown and cooked through, ensuring the internal temperature reaches 75°C (165°F).
7. Let rest for a few minutes before serving.

Nutritional Info: Calories: 400 | Fat: 20g | Carbs: 15g | Protein: 40g

ZUCCHINI NOODLES WITH PESTO

Prep: 10 mins | Cook: 5 mins | Serves: 2

Ingredients:

- **UK:** 2 medium zucchinis (spiralized), 50g gluten-free pesto, 1 tablespoon olive oil, salt, pepper, cherry tomatoes (halved for garnish)

Instructions:

1. Preheat your air fryer to 180°C (356°F).
2. Toss the spiralized zucchini with olive oil, salt, and pepper.
3. Place the zucchini noodles in the air fryer basket and cook for 3-5 minutes until just tender.
4. Remove from the air fryer, then mix in the gluten-free pesto until well coated.
5. Serve garnished with halved cherry tomatoes.

Nutritional Info: Calories: 180 | Fat: 15g | Carbs: 8g | Protein: 5g

APPLE AND BLACKBERRY CRUMBLE

Prep: 15 mins | Cook: 25 mins | Serves: 4

Ingredients:

- **UK:** 300g cooking apples (peeled, cored, and chopped), 150g blackberries, 50g gluten-free oats, 100g gluten-free flour, 50g brown sugar, 50g cold butter (cubed), 1 teaspoon cinnamon

Instructions:

1. In a bowl, combine the chopped apples and blackberries. Toss with a sprinkle of cinnamon and set aside.
2. In another bowl, mix the gluten-free oats, gluten-free flour, brown sugar, and cinnamon. Rub in the cold butter until the mixture resembles coarse crumbs.
3. Preheat your air fryer to 180°C (356°F).
4. Spoon the fruit mixture into an oven-safe dish that fits in your air fryer.
5. Top the fruit with the crumble mixture, spreading it evenly.
6. Place the dish in the air fryer basket and cook for about 25 minutes until the crumble is golden brown and the fruit is bubbling.
7. Once done, let it cool slightly before serving. It's delicious on its own or served with ice cream!

Nutritional Info: Calories: 280 | Fat: 12g | Carbs: 40g | Protein: 3g

GLUTEN-FREE CHOCOLATE LAVA CAKES

Prep: 10 mins | Cook: 12 mins | Serves: 2

Ingredients:

- **UK:** 100g dark chocolate (chopped), 50g butter, 2 eggs, 50g sugar, 30g gluten-free flour, 1 teaspoon vanilla extract

Instructions:

1. In a heatproof bowl, melt the dark chocolate and butter together in the microwave or over a saucepan of simmering water.
2. In another bowl, whisk the eggs and sugar together until light and fluffy.
3. Fold in the melted chocolate mixture, then sift in the gluten-free flour and fold until just combined.
4. Preheat your air fryer to 200°C (392°F).
5. Grease two ramekins and pour the batter evenly into them.
6. Place the ramekins in the air fryer basket and cook for about 12 minutes. The edges should be firm, while the centre remains soft.
7. Let them sit for 1 minute before inverting onto a plate. Serve immediately and enjoy the molten centre!

Nutritional Info: Calories: 360 | Fat: 25g | Carbs: 28g | Protein: 5g

CINNAMON SUGAR DOUGHNUT BITES

Prep: 20 mins | Cook: 10 mins | Serves: 4

Ingredients:

- **UK:** 200g gluten-free flour, 50g sugar, 1 teaspoon baking powder, 1 teaspoon cinnamon, 1 egg, 150ml milk, 30g melted butter

Instructions:

1. In a bowl, whisk together the gluten-free flour, sugar, baking powder, and cinnamon.
2. In another bowl, mix the egg, milk, and melted butter. Pour into the dry ingredients and stir until just combined.
3. Preheat your air fryer to 190°C (374°F).
4. Use a teaspoon to drop small balls of dough into the air fryer basket, ensuring they are spaced apart.
5. Cook for about 10 minutes until golden brown.
6. While they cool, mix sugar and cinnamon for coating. Roll each doughnut bite in the mixture.
7. Serve warm for a delightful treat!

Nutritional Info: Calories: 220 | Fat: 8g | Carbs: 34g | Protein: 4g

BAKED PEARS WITH HONEY AND WALNUTS

Prep: 10 mins | Cook: 15 mins | Serves: 2

Ingredients:

- **UK:** 2 ripe pears (halved and cored), 30ml honey, 50g walnuts (chopped), 1 teaspoon cinnamon

Instructions:

1. Preheat your air fryer to 180°C (356°F).
2. Place the pear halves in a bowl and drizzle with honey, then sprinkle with walnuts and cinnamon.
3. Arrange the pears in the air fryer basket, cut side up.
4. Cook for about 15 minutes until the pears are tender.
5. Serve warm, perhaps with a dollop of Greek yoghurt on the side!

Nutritional Info: Calories: 180 | Fat: 9g | Carbs: 27g | Protein: 2g

MINI CHEESECAKES WITH BERRY COMPOTE

Prep: 20 mins | Cook: 15 mins | Serves: 4

Ingredients:

- **UK:** 200g gluten-free digestive biscuits (crumbled), 100g cream cheese, 50g sugar, 1 teaspoon vanilla extract, 100ml double cream, 150g mixed berries (for compote)

Instructions:

1. In a bowl, mix the crumbled biscuits with melted butter to create a base. Press the mixture into the bottoms of small ramekins.
2. In another bowl, beat together the cream cheese, sugar, and vanilla extract until smooth. Fold in the double cream until well combined.
3. Spoon the cheesecake mixture over the biscuit bases.
4. Preheat your air fryer to 160°C (320°F).
5. Place the ramekins in the basket and cook for about 15 minutes. Let them cool before refrigerating for at least an hour.
6. Meanwhile, make the berry compote by gently heating the berries in a saucepan until they break down. Serve on top of the chilled cheesecakes.

Nutritional Info: Calories: 290 | Fat: 20g | Carbs: 24g | Protein: 5g

CRISPY BANANA FRITTERS

Prep: 10 mins | Cook: 15 mins | Serves: 2

Ingredients:

- **UK:** 2 ripe bananas (mashed), 100g gluten-free flour, 30g sugar, 1 teaspoon vanilla extract, 1 teaspoon baking powder, 50ml milk

Instructions:

1. In a bowl, mix the mashed bananas, gluten-free flour, sugar, vanilla extract, baking powder, and milk until you have a thick batter.
2. Preheat your air fryer to 190°C (374°F).
3. Drop spoonfuls of the batter into the air fryer basket, making sure they are not overcrowded.
4. Cook for about 15 minutes until golden brown and crispy on the outside.
5. Serve warm, dusted with icing sugar if desired.

Nutritional Info: Calories: 240 | Fat: 2g | Carbs: 48g | Protein: 4g

GLUTEN-FREE STICKY TOFFEE PUDDING

Prep: 15 mins | Cook: 25 mins | Serves: 4

Ingredients:

- **UK:** 200g gluten-free flour, 150g dates (pitted and chopped), 100g brown sugar, 100ml milk, 2 eggs, 1 teaspoon baking powder, 1 teaspoon vanilla extract

Instructions:

1. Preheat your air fryer to 160°C (320°F).
2. In a bowl, combine the chopped dates and hot water, letting them soak for about 10 minutes.
3. In another bowl, whisk the eggs, sugar, milk, and vanilla extract. Stir in the soaked dates.
4. Sift in the gluten-free flour and baking powder, and mix until just combined.
5. Pour the batter into a greased, oven-safe dish that fits in your air fryer.
6. Cook for about 25 minutes, or until a skewer comes out clean.
7. Serve warm, drizzled with a sticky toffee sauce.

Nutritional Info: Calories: 300 | Fat: 8g | Carbs: 56g | Protein: 4g

PEACH AND ALMOND TART

Prep: 15 mins | Cook: 20 mins | Serves: 4

Ingredients:

- **UK:** 200g gluten-free almond flour, 50g sugar, 100g butter (melted), 3 eggs, 2 ripe peaches (sliced), 1 teaspoon almond extract

Instructions:

1. Preheat your air fryer to 180°C (356°F).
2. In a bowl, mix together the almond flour, sugar, and melted butter. Stir in the eggs and almond extract until well combined.
3. Pour the batter into a greased tart tin or dish that fits your air fryer.
4. Arrange the peach slices on top of the batter.
5. Cook for about 20 minutes until golden and set in the middle.
6. Let it cool slightly before serving. This tart is lovely warm or at room temperature!

Nutritional Info: Calories: 310 | Fat: 22g | Carbs: 25g | Protein: 8g

CHOCOLATE CHIP COOKIE BARS

Prep: 15 mins | Cook: 20 mins | Serves: 8

Ingredients:

- **UK:** 200g gluten-free flour, 100g butter (softened), 100g brown sugar, 50g granulated sugar, 1 egg, 1 teaspoon vanilla extract, 100g chocolate chips

Instructions:

1. Preheat your air fryer to 160°C (320°F).
2. In a bowl, cream together the softened butter, brown sugar, and granulated sugar until smooth.
3. Beat in the egg and vanilla extract until well combined.
4. Gradually stir in the gluten-free flour and fold in the chocolate chips.
5. Spread the mixture into a greased baking dish that fits your air fryer.
6. Cook for about 20 minutes until golden brown and a skewer comes out clean.
7. Let cool before cutting into bars.

Nutritional Info: Calories: 250 | Fat: 12g | Carbs: 35g | Protein: 3g

LEMON DRIZZLE CAKE SQUARES

Prep: 15 mins | Cook: 25 mins | Serves: 6

Ingredients:

- **UK:** 200g gluten-free flour, 150g sugar, 100g butter (softened), 3 eggs, zest and juice of 1 lemon, 1 teaspoon baking powder

Instructions:

1. Preheat your air fryer to 160°C (320°F).
2. In a bowl, beat together the softened butter and sugar until light and fluffy.
3. Add the eggs, lemon zest, and juice, mixing until combined.
4. Sift in the gluten-free flour and baking powder, folding gently until just combined.
5. Pour the mixture into a greased baking dish that fits your air fryer.
6. Cook for about 25 minutes or until golden and a skewer comes out clean.
7. Allow to cool slightly, then drizzle with a mix of lemon juice and icing sugar before slicing into squares.

Nutritional Info: Calories: 220 | Fat: 10g | Carbs: 30g | Protein: 4g

HOMEMADE TOMATO KETCHUP

Prep: 10 mins | Cook: 15 mins | Serves: 500ml

Ingredients:

- **UK:** 400g canned tomatoes, 50g onion (finely chopped), 2 cloves garlic (minced), 30ml apple cider vinegar, 20g brown sugar, 1 teaspoon salt, 1/2 teaspoon black pepper, 1/2 teaspoon paprika

Instructions:

1. Blend the base: In a blender, combine the canned tomatoes, onion, garlic, apple cider vinegar, brown sugar, salt, black pepper, and paprika. Blend until smooth.
2. Cook in the air fryer: Pour the blended mixture into an air fryer-safe dish. Set the air fryer to 160°C (320°F) and cook for 15 minutes, stirring halfway through to prevent sticking.
3. Check consistency: After cooking, check the ketchup. If it's too runny, air fry for an additional 5 minutes, checking frequently.
4. Cool and store: Allow the ketchup to cool before transferring it to a jar. Store it in the fridge for up to two weeks.
5. Enjoy your homemade ketchup with fries or burgers!

Nutritional Info: Calories: 50 | Fat: 0g | Carbs: 12g | Protein: 2g

GLUTEN-FREE BARBECUE SAUCE

Prep: 5 mins | Cook: 10 mins | Serves: 300ml

Ingredients:

- **UK:** 240ml tomato sauce, 30ml apple cider vinegar, 30g brown sugar, 1 tablespoon Worcestershire sauce, 1 teaspoon smoked paprika, 1 teaspoon garlic powder, salt, pepper to taste

Instructions:

1. Mix the ingredients: In a bowl, whisk together the tomato sauce, apple cider vinegar, brown sugar, Worcestershire sauce, smoked paprika, garlic powder, salt, and pepper.
2. Cook in the air fryer: Transfer the mixture into an air fryer-safe dish. Set the air fryer to 160°C (320°F) and cook for 10 minutes, stirring halfway through.
3. Taste and adjust: After cooking, taste the sauce and adjust the seasoning if necessary.
4. Cool and store: Let it cool before pouring into a bottle. Store in the fridge for up to one month.
5. Use this BBQ sauce to elevate your grilled meats or veggies!

Nutritional Info: Calories: 70 | Fat: 0g | Carbs: 18g | Protein: 1g

GARLIC AIOLI

Prep: 10 mins | Cook: 0 mins | Serves: 200ml

Ingredients:

- **UK:** 100g mayonnaise, 2 cloves garlic (minced), 10ml lemon juice, 1 teaspoon Dijon mustard, salt to taste

Instructions:

1. Combine the ingredients: In a bowl, mix the mayonnaise, minced garlic, lemon juice, Dijon mustard, and salt until smooth.
2. Chill: Cover and refrigerate for at least 30 minutes to allow the flavors to meld.
3. Serve: Use as a dip for chips or as a spread for sandwiches.
4. Keep refrigerated: Store any leftovers in an airtight container in the fridge for up to one week.

Nutritional Info: Calories: 90 | Fat: 10g | Carbs: 1g | Protein: 1g

SWEET CHILLI SAUCE

Prep: 5 mins | Cook: 15 mins | Serves: 300ml

Ingredients:

- **UK:** 100g sugar, 60ml water, 30ml rice vinegar, 2 teaspoons soy sauce, 2 teaspoons cornstarch, 1 teaspoon red chili flakes

Instructions:

1. Prepare the sauce: In a saucepan, combine the sugar, water, rice vinegar, soy sauce, and red chili flakes. Heat over medium until the sugar dissolves.
2. Thicken the sauce: In a small bowl, mix the cornstarch with a bit of cold water to form a slurry. Slowly whisk it into the saucepan.
3. Air fry to cook: Pour the sauce into an air fryer-safe dish and set the air fryer to 180°C (356°F). Cook for 10 minutes, stirring halfway through.
4. Cool and bottle: Once thickened, let it cool before transferring to a bottle. Store in the fridge for up to one month.
5. Perfect for dipping spring rolls or drizzling over grilled meats!

Nutritional Info: Calories: 120 | Fat: 0g | Carbs: 31g | Protein: 0g

MINT YOGHURT DIP

Prep: 5 mins | Cook: 0 mins | Serves: 200ml

Ingredients:

- **UK:** 200g Greek yogurt, 1 tablespoon fresh mint (chopped), 1 tablespoon lemon juice, salt to taste

Instructions:

1. Mix the ingredients: In a bowl, combine the Greek yogurt, chopped mint, lemon juice, and salt. Stir until well mixed.
2. Chill: Refrigerate for at least 30 minutes before serving to let the flavors meld.
3. Serve: This dip pairs wonderfully with grilled meats or as a veggie dip.
4. Store in the fridge: Use within one week for the best flavor.

Nutritional Info: Calories: 60 | Fat: 4g | Carbs: 3g | Protein: 5g

CRANBERRY AND ORANGE SAUCE

Prep: 10 mins | Cook: 20 mins | Serves: 400ml

Ingredients:

- **UK:** 200g fresh cranberries, 100g sugar, 150ml orange juice, zest of 1 orange

Instructions:

1. Prepare the mixture: In a saucepan, combine the cranberries, sugar, orange juice, and orange zest.
2. Cook until bubbly: Bring to a boil, then reduce the heat and simmer for about 20 minutes, stirring occasionally until thickened.
3. Cool and store: Allow to cool before transferring to a jar. This sauce can be refrigerated for up to two weeks.
4. Use as a festive side for meats or spread on toast!

Nutritional Info: Calories: 100 | Fat: 0g | Carbs: 25g | Protein: 0g

GLUTEN-FREE GRAVY

Prep: 5 mins | Cook: 15 mins | Serves: 400ml

Ingredients:

- **UK:** 500ml chicken or vegetable stock, 30g gluten-free flour, 30g butter, salt, and pepper to taste

Instructions:

1. Melt the butter: In a saucepan, melt the butter over medium heat.
2. Make a roux: Whisk in the gluten-free flour until it forms a paste and cook for 1-2 minutes.
3. Add the stock: Gradually whisk in the stock, ensuring no lumps form.
4. Thicken in the air fryer: Pour the gravy into an air fryer-safe dish and set the air fryer to 180°C (356°F) for about 10-15 minutes, stirring halfway until thickened.
5. Season and serve: Adjust seasoning with salt and pepper before serving over your favorite dishes.

Nutritional Info: Calories: 90 | Fat: 5g | Carbs: 10g | Protein: 1g

HONEY MUSTARD DRESSING

Prep: 5 mins | Cook: 0 mins | Serves: 200ml

Ingredients:

- **UK:** 50ml honey, 50ml Dijon mustard, 50ml apple cider vinegar, 30ml olive oil, salt and pepper to taste

Instructions:

1. Combine the ingredients: In a jar, combine the honey, Dijon mustard, apple cider vinegar, and olive oil.
2. Shake well: Secure the lid and shake vigorously until well combined.
3. Taste and adjust: Taste the dressing and adjust seasoning with salt and pepper as desired.
4. Serve: Drizzle over salads or use as a dipping sauce.
5. Store in the fridge: This dressing will keep for up to two weeks.

Nutritional Info: Calories: 70 | Fat: 3g | Carbs: 10g | Protein: 1g

TZATZIKI SAUCE

Prep: 10 mins | Cook: 0 mins | Serves: 250ml

Ingredients:

- **UK:** 200g Greek yogurt, 1 cucumber (grated), 1 clove garlic (minced), 10ml lemon juice, salt, and pepper to taste

Instructions:

1. Grate the cucumber: Grate the cucumber and squeeze out excess moisture using a clean cloth or paper towel.
2. Mix the ingredients: In a bowl, combine the Greek yogurt, grated cucumber, minced garlic, lemon juice, and salt.
3. Chill before serving: Refrigerate for at least 30 minutes to allow flavors to develop.
4. Serve as a dip: This is great with pita bread or as a side to grilled meats.
5. Store in the fridge: Use within one week for the best flavor.

Nutritional Info: Calories: 50 | Fat: 4g | Carbs: 3g | Protein: 3g

MANGO CHUTNEY

Prep: 10 mins | Cook: 20 mins | Serves: 300ml

Ingredients:

- **UK:** 300g ripe mango (peeled and diced), 100g sugar, 50ml apple cider vinegar, 1 teaspoon grated ginger, 1 teaspoon chili flakes

Instructions:

1. Combine the ingredients: In a saucepan, mix the diced mango, sugar, apple cider vinegar, grated ginger, and chili flakes.
2. Cook down: Bring to a boil, then reduce heat and simmer for about 20 minutes, stirring occasionally until thickened.
3. Cool and jar: Allow to cool before transferring to a jar. This chutney can be refrigerated for up to one month.
4. Perfect as a condiment: Serve alongside curries or grilled meats for a sweet and spicy kick.

Nutritional Info: Calories: 120 | Fat: 0g | Carbs: 31g | Protein: 1g

AIR FRYER FALAFEL

Prep: 15 mins | Cook: 15 mins | Serves: 4

Ingredients:

- **UK:** 400g canned chickpeas (drained and rinsed), 1 small onion (chopped), 2 cloves garlic (minced), 1 teaspoon ground cumin, 1 teaspoon ground coriander, 30g fresh parsley (chopped), 30g fresh coriander (chopped), 60g gluten-free flour, salt, pepper, cooking spray

Instructions:

1. In a food processor, combine the chickpeas, onion, garlic, cumin, coriander, parsley, cilantro, gluten-free flour, salt, and pepper. Pulse until coarsely blended, but not puréed.
2. Form the mixture into small balls or patties, about the size of a golf ball.
3. Preheat your air fryer to 180°C (350°F) for 5 minutes.
4. Lightly spray the air fryer basket with cooking spray. Place the falafel balls in the basket in a single layer, ensuring they don't touch.
5. Cook for 12-15 minutes, flipping halfway through, until golden brown and crispy.
6. Serve warm with tahini sauce or a fresh salad. Enjoy your crispy falafel!

Nutritional Info: Calories: 220 | Fat: 6g | Carbs: 32g | Protein: 10g

STUFFED BELL PEPPERS WITH QUINOA

Prep: 20 mins | Cook: 25 mins | Serves: 4

Ingredients:

- **UK:** 4 large bell peppers (halved and seeds removed), 200g cooked quinoa, 100g black beans (drained and rinsed), 1 small onion (chopped), 2 cloves garlic (minced), 1 teaspoon cumin, 200g diced tomatoes, 30g nutritional yeast, salt, pepper, cooking spray

Instructions:

1. In a bowl, mix cooked quinoa, black beans, onion, garlic, cumin, diced tomatoes, nutritional yeast, salt, and pepper until combined.
2. Preheat your air fryer to 190°C (375°F) for 5 minutes.
3. Stuff each bell pepper half with the quinoa mixture, pressing down lightly to pack it in.
4. Lightly spray the air fryer basket and arrange the stuffed peppers inside.
5. Cook for 20-25 minutes until the peppers are tender and the tops are slightly crispy.
6. Serve warm, garnished with fresh herbs if desired. Enjoy your nutritious stuffed peppers!

Nutritional Info: Calories: 180 | Fat: 3g | Carbs: 32g | Protein: 8g

VEGAN CHICKPEA NUGGETS

Prep: 10 mins | Cook: 15 mins | Serves: 4

Ingredients:

- **UK:** 400g canned chickpeas (drained and rinsed), 50g gluten-free breadcrumbs, 1 teaspoon garlic powder, 1 teaspoon onion powder, 1 teaspoon paprika, salt, pepper, cooking spray

Instructions:

1. In a mixing bowl, mash the chickpeas with a fork until mostly smooth. Stir in breadcrumbs, garlic powder, onion powder, paprika, salt, and pepper until well combined.
2. Preheat your air fryer to 200°C (400°F) for 5 minutes.
3. Shape the mixture into small nugget shapes.
4. Lightly spray the air fryer basket and arrange the nuggets in a single layer.
5. Cook for 12-15 minutes, flipping halfway through until golden and crispy.
6. Serve with your favourite dipping sauce. Enjoy your chickpea nuggets!

Nutritional Info: Calories: 210 | Fat: 5g | Carbs: 30g | Protein: 9g

CRISPY TOFU WITH PEANUT SAUCE

Prep: 15 mins | Cook: 20 mins | Serves: 4

Ingredients:

- **UK:** 400g firm tofu (pressed and cubed), 30ml soy sauce, 1 tablespoon cornstarch, 60ml peanut butter, 1 tablespoon maple syrup, 1 tablespoon rice vinegar, 1 clove garlic (minced), water to thin, chopped peanuts and spring onions (for garnish)

Instructions:

1. In a bowl, toss the cubed tofu with soy sauce and cornstarch until evenly coated.
2. Preheat your air fryer to 200°C (400°F) for 5 minutes.
3. Lightly spray the basket and arrange the tofu cubes in a single layer.
4. Cook for 15-20 minutes, shaking the basket halfway through until the tofu is golden and crispy.
5. Meanwhile, whisk together peanut butter, maple syrup, rice vinegar, garlic, and enough water to reach your desired sauce consistency.
6. Serve the crispy tofu drizzled with peanut sauce and garnished with chopped peanuts and spring onions. Enjoy!

Nutritional Info: Calories: 350 | Fat: 25g | Carbs: 20g | Protein: 15g

PORTOBELLO MUSHROOM BURGERS

Prep: 10 mins | Cook: 15 mins | Serves: 4

Ingredients:

- **UK:** 4 large portobello mushrooms (stems removed), 60ml balsamic vinegar, 30ml olive oil, 1 teaspoon garlic powder, salt, pepper, gluten-free burger buns, lettuce, tomato, and avocado (for serving)

Instructions:

1. In a bowl, whisk together balsamic vinegar, olive oil, garlic powder, salt, and pepper.
2. Marinate the portobello mushrooms in the mixture for at least 10 minutes.
3. Preheat your air fryer to 200°C (400°F) for 5 minutes.
4. Place the marinated mushrooms in the basket and cook for 10-15 minutes until tender and juicy.
5. Assemble your burgers with the cooked mushrooms, lettuce, tomato, and avocado on gluten-free buns. Enjoy your hearty mushroom burgers!

Nutritional Info: Calories: 280 | Fat: 15g | Carbs: 30g | Protein: 8g

EGGPLANT PARMESAN

Prep: 20 mins | Cook: 25 mins | Serves: 4

Ingredients:

- **UK:** 1 large eggplant (sliced into rounds), 200g gluten-free breadcrumbs, 2 eggs (beaten), 400g marinara sauce, 150g mozzarella cheese (shredded), 30g grated Parmesan cheese, salt, pepper, cooking spray

Instructions:

1. Season the eggplant slices with salt and let sit for 10 minutes to draw out moisture. Pat dry.
2. Dip each slice in beaten eggs, then coat in gluten-free breadcrumbs.
3. Preheat your air fryer to 200°C (400°F) for 5 minutes.
4. Lightly spray the basket and arrange the breaded eggplant slices in a single layer.
5. Cook for 15 minutes until golden brown and crispy.
6. In a baking dish, layer the eggplant, marinara sauce, mozzarella, and Parmesan. Repeat until all ingredients are used, finishing with cheese on top.
7. Return to the air fryer and cook for an additional 10 minutes until bubbly and golden. Enjoy your eggplant Parmesan!

Nutritional Info: Calories: 320 | Fat: 18g | Carbs: 30g | Protein: 12g

STUFFED ACORN SQUASH

Prep: 20 mins | Cook: 30 mins | Serves: 4

Ingredients:

- **UK:** 2 acorn squashes (halved and seeds removed), 200g cooked quinoa, 100g cranberries, 30g pecans (chopped), 1 teaspoon cinnamon, salt, pepper, cooking spray

Instructions:

1. Preheat your air fryer to 190°C (375°F) for 5 minutes.
2. In a bowl, mix cooked quinoa, cranberries, pecans, cinnamon, salt, and pepper until combined.
3. Stuff each squash half with the quinoa mixture, pressing down lightly to pack it in.
4. Lightly spray the air fryer basket and place the stuffed squashes inside.
5. Cook for 25-30 minutes until the squashes are tender and the tops are slightly crispy. Enjoy your delicious stuffed acorn squash!

Nutritional Info: Calories: 250 | Fat: 7g | Carbs: 40g | Protein: 8g

VEGGIE SPRING ROLLS

Prep: 15 mins | Cook: 10 mins | Serves: 4

Ingredients:

- **UK:** 8 rice paper wrappers, 200g mixed vegetables (carrot, cucumber, bell pepper, sliced), 30g fresh mint leaves, 30g fresh coriander, 30ml soy sauce (for dipping), cooking spray

Instructions:

1. Soak rice paper wrappers in warm water for about 10 seconds until softened. Lay on a clean surface.
2. Place a small amount of mixed vegetables and herbs at the bottom of each wrapper and roll tightly, tucking in the sides as you go.
3. Preheat your air fryer to 180°C (350°F) for 5 minutes.
4. Lightly spray the air fryer basket and arrange the spring rolls in a single layer.
5. Cook for 8-10 minutes until crispy and golden brown. Serve with soy sauce for dipping. Enjoy your fresh spring rolls!

Nutritional Info: Calories: 150 | Fat: 4g | Carbs: 25g | Protein: 3g

BUTTERNUT SQUASH FRITTERS

Prep: 15 mins | Cook: 15 mins | Serves: 4

Ingredients:

- **UK:** 400g butternut squash (peeled and grated), 50g gluten-free flour, 1 teaspoon garlic powder, 1 egg (beaten), salt, pepper, cooking spray

Instructions:

1. In a bowl, mix grated butternut squash, gluten-free flour, garlic powder, beaten egg, salt, and pepper until well combined.
2. Preheat your air fryer to 200°C (400°F) for 5 minutes.
3. Lightly spray the basket and spoon dollops of the mixture to form fritters.
4. Cook for 12-15 minutes, flipping halfway through until golden and crispy. Enjoy your delicious fritters!

Nutritional Info: Calories: 220 | Fat: 5g | Carbs: 38g | Protein: 6g

CRISPY BRUSSELS SPROUTS

Prep: 10 mins | Cook: 15 mins | Serves: 4

Ingredients:

- **UK:** 500g Brussels sprouts (halved), 30ml olive oil, 1 teaspoon garlic powder, salt, pepper, cooking spray

Instructions:

1. In a bowl, toss halved Brussels sprouts with olive oil, garlic powder, salt, and pepper until evenly coated.
2. Preheat your air fryer to 200°C (400°F) for 5 minutes.
3. Lightly spray the basket and add the Brussels sprouts in a single layer.
4. Cook for 12-15 minutes until crispy and browned, shaking the basket halfway through. Enjoy your crispy Brussels sprouts!

Nutritional Info: Calories: 150 | Fat: 8g | Carbs: 15g | Protein: 5g

PRODUCE:

- Apples
- Blackberries
- Lemons
- Limes
- Oranges
- Bell peppers (variety of colours)
- Garlic
- Onions (white, red, and green)
- Carrots
- Courgettes
- Sweet potatoes
- Brussels sprouts
- Green beans
- Cauliflower
- Broccoli
- Butternut squash
- Acorn squash
- Mushrooms (Portobello and white button)
- Fresh herbs (parsley, rosemary, thyme, mint, basil)
- Spinach
- Kale
- Dill
- Aubergine (eggplant)
- Potatoes
- Tomatoes (for cooking and sauces)
- Avocado
- Berries (strawberries, raspberries, blueberries)
- Bananas
- Peaches
- Cranberries
- Mediterranean vegetables (courgette, aubergine, peppers)

MEAT AND POULTRY:

- Chicken breasts
- Chicken thighs
- Chicken drumsticks
- Chicken wings
- Turkey breast
- Ground turkey
- Gammon (ham)
- Bacon
- Pork belly
- Beef tenderloin
- Lamb rack
- Cornish hens
- Ground beef
- Sausages (gluten-free)
- Fish (salmon fillets, white fish like cod for fish and chips)
- Lobster tails

DAIRY AND EGGS:

- Eggs
- Butter (unsalted and salted)
- Cream cheese
- Parmesan cheese
- Cheddar cheese
- Mozzarella cheese
- Halloumi
- Greek yoghurt
- Milk (dairy or dairy-free alternatives)
- Cream (heavy and light)
- Coconut milk (optional for vegan dishes)

PANTRY ITEMS:

- Gluten-free flour
- Gluten-free bread crumbs
- Gluten-free pasta
- Gluten-free crumpets
- Gluten-free oats
- Gluten-free flatbread or tortillas
- Gluten-free baking powder
- Gluten-free soy sauce
- Quinoa
- Rice (white and brown)
- Polenta
- Canned chickpeas
- Canned tomatoes
- Coconut oil
- Olive oil
- Vegetable oil
- Honey

- Maple syrup
- Peanut butter
- Almond butter
- Coconut sugar
- Brown sugar
- White sugar
- Cocoa powder (gluten-free)
- Baking soda
- Cornstarch
- Ground cinnamon
- Ground nutmeg
- Ground cumin
- Ground paprika (regular and smoked)
- Ground turmeric
- Chilli flakes
- Dried oregano
- Dried basil
- Ground mustard
- Salt
- Black pepper
- Balsamic vinegar
- White wine vinegar
- Red wine vinegar
- Apple cider vinegar
- Gluten-free BBQ sauce
- Gluten-free gravy mix
- Tomato ketchup
- Mustard (Dijon, honey mustard)
- Tomato paste
- Coconut flakes

- Almond flour
- Chia seeds
- Pumpkin seeds
- Sunflower seeds
- Gluten-free breadcrumbs
- Almond meal
- Nut butter (optional)
- Maple syrup
- Golden syrup
- Sesame seeds
- Dried cranberries
- Sultanas
- Chocolate chips (gluten-free)
- Dark chocolate (gluten-free)

FROZEN SECTION:

- Frozen berries (for smoothies, desserts)
- Frozen peas
- Frozen mixed vegetables
- Frozen chips (gluten-free option for air fryer)

CONDIMENTS AND SAUCES:

- Honey mustard dressing
- Cranberry and orange sauce
- Sweet chilli sauce
- Garlic aioli
- Tzatziki sauce
- Mango chutney

This list covers the essentials for creating your gluten-free air fryer meals. Feel free to adjust quantities based on your specific recipe needs.

Here's a 60-day meal plan to help you get the most out of your gluten-free air fryer. The plan includes a variety of breakfast, lunch, dinner, and snack options, ensuring you enjoy a well-balanced and delicious diet.

DAY	BREAKFAST	LUNCH	DINNER	SNACK
1	Cheesy Spinach and Mushroom Frittata	Crispy Halloumi Fries	Herb-Crusted Roast Chicken	Sweet and Spicy Mixed Nuts
2	Sweet Potato and Kale Breakfast Hash	Gluten-Free Sausage Rolls	Gluten-Free Fish and Chips	Cinnamon Apple Breakfast Crisps
3	Gluten-Free Crumpets	Crispy Vegetable Pakoras	Stuffed Bell Peppers with Quinoa and Black Beans	Garlic and Herb Mushrooms
4	Smoked Salmon and Dill Frittata	Spicy Chickpea Poppers	Lemon and Garlic Salmon Fillets	Homemade Potato Crisps with Sea Salt
5	Berry and Oat Breakfast Bars	Gluten-Free Onion Bhajis	Crispy Pork Belly with Apple Sauce	Cinnamon Rolls with Cream Cheese Frosting
6	Gluten-Free Breakfast Sausage Patties	Crispy Coconut Prawns	Vegetable and Chickpea Curry	Gluten-Free Chocolate Chip Cookies
7	Bacon and Egg Cups	Garlic Knots	Gluten-Free Chicken Kiev	Baked Pears with Honey and Walnuts
8	Crispy Hash Browns	Sesame Bagels	Stuffed Portobello Mushrooms	Mini Cheesecakes with Berry Compote
9	Full English Breakfast Stack	Cheddar Biscuits	Honey and Mustard Glazed Gammon	Crispy Banana Fritters
10	Cinnamon Apple Breakfast Crisps	Herb and Garlic Flatbread	Crispy Tofu Stir-Fry	Gluten-Free Sticky Toffee Pudding
11	Gluten-Free Banana Bread	Spicy Chickpea Poppers	Lemon Garlic Chicken Drumsticks	Sweet and Spicy Mixed Nuts
12	Sweet Potato and Kale Breakfast Hash	Garlic and Herb Mushrooms	Honey Mustard Chicken Thighs	Cinnamon Sugar Doughnut Bites
13	Cheesy Spinach and Mushroom Frittata	Homemade Potato Crisps with Sea Salt	Cajun Chicken Tenders	Gluten-Free Chocolate Lava Cakes
14	Smoked Salmon and Dill Frittata	Rosemary Olive Oil Focaccia	BBQ Chicken Wings	Peach and Almond Tart

DAY	BREAKFAST	LUNCH	DINNER	SNACK
15	Bacon and Egg Cups	Sweet Potato Wedges	Crispy Chicken Breast with Herbs	Gluten-Free Chocolate Chip Cookie Bars
16	Cinnamon Rolls with Cream Cheese Frosting	Crispy Brussels Sprouts with Balsamic Glaze	Garlic Parmesan Chicken Nuggets	Apple and Blackberry Crumble
17	Gluten-Free Crumpets	Cheddar Biscuits	Teriyaki Chicken Skewers	Baked Pears with Honey and Walnuts
18	Gluten-Free Breakfast Sausage Patties	Roasted Mediterranean Vegetables	Rosemary Roast Turkey Breast	Lemon Drizzle Cake Squares
19	Full English Breakfast Stack	Garlic and Parmesan Courgette Fries	Greek Lemon Chicken Souvlaki	Crispy Coconut Prawns
20	Cheesy Spinach and Mushroom Frittata	Spicy Chickpea Poppers	Buffalo Chicken Tenders	Sweet and Spicy Mixed Nuts
21	Sweet Potato and Kale Breakfast Hash	Crispy Halloumi Fries	Gluten-Free Chicken Kiev	Mini Cheesecakes with Berry Compote
22	Berry and Oat Breakfast Bars	Gluten-Free Onion Bhajis	Herb-Crusted Roast Chicken	Cinnamon Rolls with Cream Cheese Frosting
23	Bacon and Egg Cups	Garlic Knots	Honey and Mustard Glazed Gammon	Crispy Banana Fritters
24	Gluten-Free Crumpets	Sweet Potato Wedges	Lemon and Garlic Salmon Fillets	Gluten-Free Sticky Toffee Pudding
25	Crispy Hash Browns	Sesame Bagels	Cajun Chicken Tenders	Baked Pears with Honey and Walnuts
26	Cinnamon Apple Breakfast Crisps	Herb and Garlic Flatbread	Teriyaki Chicken Skewers	Gluten-Free Chocolate Lava Cakes
27	Gluten-Free Banana Bread	Spicy Chickpea Poppers	Rosemary Roast Turkey Breast	Peach and Almond Tart
28	Full English Breakfast Stack	Crispy Vegetable Pakoras	Greek Lemon Chicken Souvlaki	Sweet and Spicy Mixed Nuts
29	Smoked Salmon and Dill Frittata	Garlic and Herb Mushrooms	Crispy Chicken Breast with Herbs	Gluten-Free Chocolate Chip Cookie Bars
30	Cheesy Spinach and Mushroom Frittata	Sweet Potato Wedges	Buffalo Chicken Tenders	Cinnamon Sugar Doughnut Bites
31	Sweet Potato and Kale Breakfast Hash	Homemade Potato Crisps with Sea Salt	Lemon Garlic Chicken Drumsticks	Gluten-Free Chocolate Lava Cakes

DAY	BREAKFAST	LUNCH	DINNER	SNACK
32	Berry and Oat Breakfast Bars	Gluten-Free Onion Bhajis	Honey Mustard Chicken Thighs	Baked Pears with Honey and Walnuts
33	Bacon and Egg Cups	Crispy Halloumi Fries	Crispy Pork Belly with Apple Sauce	Mini Cheesecakes with Berry Compote
34	Gluten-Free Crumpets	Garlic Knots	Stuffed Bell Peppers with Quinoa and Black Beans	Gluten-Free Chocolate Chip Cookies
35	Cinnamon Apple Breakfast Crisps	Garlic and Parmesan Courgette Fries	Teriyaki Chicken Skewers	Apple and Blackberry Crumble
36	Gluten-Free Breakfast Sausage Patties	Roasted Mediterranean Vegetables	Crispy Chicken Breast with Herbs	Lemon Drizzle Cake Squares
37	Full English Breakfast Stack	Spicy Chickpea Poppers	Buffalo Chicken Tenders	Peach and Almond Tart
38	Cheesy Spinach and Mushroom Frittata	Crispy Coconut Prawns	Herb-Crusted Roast Chicken	Cinnamon Sugar Doughnut Bites
39	Bacon and Egg Cups	Gluten-Free Onion Bhajis	Honey and Mustard Glazed Gammon	Sweet and Spicy Mixed Nuts
40	Smoked Salmon and Dill Frittata	Sesame Bagels	Cajun Chicken Tenders	Baked Pears with Honey and Walnuts
41	Sweet Potato and Kale Breakfast Hash	Garlic and Herb Mushrooms	Lemon Garlic Chicken Drumsticks	Mini Cheesecakes with Berry Compote
42	Gluten-Free Crumpets	Sweet Potato Wedges	Greek Lemon Chicken Souvlaki	Cinnamon Rolls with Cream Cheese Frosting
43	Crispy Hash Browns	Crispy Brussels Sprouts with Balsamic Glaze	Buffalo Chicken Tenders	Gluten-Free Chocolate Chip Cookie Bars
44	Cinnamon Apple Breakfast Crisps	Garlic Knots	Stuffed Bell Peppers with Quinoa and Black Beans	Gluten-Free Chocolate Lava Cakes
45	Gluten-Free Banana Bread	Crispy Coconut Prawns	Honey Mustard Chicken Thighs	Peach and Almond Tart
46	Full English Breakfast Stack	Sweet Potato Wedges	Crispy Pork Belly with Apple Sauce	Sweet and Spicy Mixed Nuts
47	Berry and Oat Breakfast Bars	Herb and Garlic Flatbread	Teriyaki Chicken Skewers	Baked Pears with Honey and Walnuts

DAY	BREAKFAST	LUNCH	DINNER	SNACK
48	Gluten-Free Crumpets	Roasted Mediterranean Vegetables	Crispy Chicken Breast with Herbs	Mini Cheesecakes with Berry Compote
49	Cheesy Spinach and Mushroom Frittata	Spicy Chickpea Poppers	Herb-Crusted Roast Chicken	Gluten-Free Chocolate Chip Cookies
50	Bacon and Egg Cups	Garlic and Herb Mushrooms	Lemon and Garlic Salmon Fillets	Cinnamon Rolls with Cream Cheese Frosting
51	Cinnamon Apple Breakfast Crisps	Garlic Knots	Cajun Chicken Tenders	Sweet and Spicy Mixed Nuts
52	Sweet Potato and Kale Breakfast Hash	Crispy Vegetable Pakoras	Crispy Tofu Stir-Fry	Gluten-Free Chocolate Lava Cakes
53	Gluten-Free Breakfast Sausage Patties	Sweet Potato Wedges	Greek Lemon Chicken Souvlaki	Baked Pears with Honey and Walnuts
54	Full English Breakfast Stack	Garlic and Parmesan Courgette Fries	Crispy Pork Belly with Apple Sauce	Mini Cheesecakes with Berry Compote
55	Berry and Oat Breakfast Bars	Homemade Potato Crisps with Sea Salt	Buffalo Chicken Tenders	Gluten-Free Chocolate Chip Cookies
56	Smoked Salmon and Dill Frittata	Crispy Halloumi Fries	Herb-Crusted Roast Chicken	Cinnamon Sugar Doughnut Bites
57	Gluten-Free Banana Bread	Gluten-Free Onion Bhajis	Lemon Garlic Chicken Drumsticks	Sweet and Spicy Mixed Nuts
58	Cheesy Spinach and Mushroom Frittata	Spicy Chickpea Poppers	Honey Mustard Chicken Thighs	Gluten-Free Chocolate Lava Cakes
59	Bacon and Egg Cups	Garlic and Herb Mushrooms	Cajun Chicken Tenders	Baked Pears with Honey and Walnuts
60	Sweet Potato and Kale Breakfast Hash	Garlic Knots	Crispy Tofu Stir-Fry	Mini Cheesecakes with Berry Compote

This 60-day meal plan combines variety, flavour, and balance, ensuring you get the most from your gluten-free air fryer without compromising on taste or convenience.

CONCLUSION

As we come to the end of this culinary journey, it's clear that the combination of gluten-free cooking and air frying has opened up a world of delicious possibilities. Throughout this cookbook, we've explored how to create a wide array of mouthwatering dishes that cater to those with gluten sensitivities or celiac disease, all while harnessing the power and convenience of the air fryer.

From crispy appetizers to hearty main courses, from delightful sides to indulgent desserts, we've discovered that living gluten-free doesn't mean sacrificing flavor or texture. The air fryer has proven to be an invaluable tool in creating dishes that are not only safe for those avoiding gluten but are also crispy, tender, and full of flavor – often rivaling or surpassing their gluten-containing counterparts.

We've learned that air frying is not just about creating healthier versions of fried foods. It's a versatile cooking method that can roast, bake, and even grill, all while using minimal oil and reducing cooking times. This makes it an ideal companion for busy individuals and families looking to prepare quick, nutritious, and delicious gluten-free meals.

Throughout the recipes, we've explored a variety of cuisines and cooking styles, demonstrating that gluten-free air frying can accommodate diverse tastes and dietary preferences. Whether you're craving comfort food like crispy chicken tenders, exploring international flavors with falafel or spring rolls, or satisfying your sweet tooth with cinnamon rolls or lava cakes, there's a gluten-free air fryer recipe to suit every palate.

We've also delved into the basics of gluten-free cooking, providing you with the knowledge and confidence to adapt recipes and create your own gluten-free masterpieces. From understanding gluten-free flours and binding agents to mastering the art of breading without wheat, you now have the tools to experiment and innovate in your kitchen.

The air fryer has shown its worth not just in everyday cooking, but also for special occasions. We've explored recipes that can impress guests at dinner parties or make holiday meals extra special, all while keeping them safe for those with gluten sensitivities.

Remember, the journey doesn't end here. Use this cookbook as a starting point for your own culinary adventures. Don't be afraid to experiment with different ingredients, adjust seasonings to your taste, or even combine elements from different recipes to create your own signature dishes.

As you continue your gluten-free air frying journey, keep these key points in mind:

1. Always check your ingredients to ensure they're certified gluten-free.

2. Experiment with different gluten-free flours and starches to achieve the perfect texture.

3. Use the air fryer's temperature controls and timing to your advantage for optimal results.

4. Don't forget to preheat your air fryer for the crispiest results.

5. Clean your air fryer regularly to maintain its performance and prevent cross-contamination.

We've provided you with bonus materials – a comprehensive grocery list and a 60-day gastric sleeve bariatric meal plan – to help you integrate these recipes into your daily life seamlessly. Use these tools to make meal planning easier and ensure you always have the right ingredients on hand for your next gluten-free air fryer creation.

Whether you're new to gluten-free cooking, a long-time air fryer enthusiast, or somewhere in between, we hope this cookbook has inspired you to explore new flavors, textures, and techniques. Cooking should be a joy, not a chore, and we believe that with your air fryer and these recipes, you'll find plenty of joy in creating delicious, gluten-free meals for yourself, your family, and your friends.

So, preheat that air fryer, gather your ingredients, and let your culinary creativity soar. Here's to many more delicious, gluten-free meals made easy and enjoyable with your trusty air fryer. **Happy cooking!**

Printed in Great Britain
by Amazon

54872748R00046